The Mini**FARMING**™
Guide to
Composting

The Mini **FARMING**™
Guide to
Composting

Brett L. Markham

Skyhorse Publishing

Skyhorse Publishing books may be purchased in bulk at special discounts for sales promotion, corporate gifts, fund-raising, or educational purposes. Special editions can also be created to specifications. For details, contact the Special Sales Department, Skyhorse Publishing, 307 West 36th Street, 11th Floor, New York, NY 10018 or info@skyhorsepublishing.com.

Skyhorse® and Skyhorse Publishing® are registered trademarks of Skyhorse Publishing, Inc.®, a Delaware corporation.

www.skyhorsepublishing.com

10 9 8 7 6 5 4 3

Library of Congress Cataloging-in-Publication Data is available on file.

ISBN: 978-1-61608-858-3

Printed in China

Table of Contents

Acknowledgments

Over the past couple of years since the release of *Mini Farming: Self Sufficiency on ¼ Acre*, I've had a lot of contact with my readers. I've received questions and feedback from all over the world via my website at www.markhamfarm.com. I knew that the book had been translated into German, but was pleasantly surprised to discover I have readers in places like Malaysia. I've also been invited to speak in numerous venues and the question and answer sessions have often been as enlightening to me as the audience. People interested in organic gardening or self-sufficiency tend to be independent thinkers, so sometimes they've made me go, "Hey! That's great! I never thought about it that way."

I had addressed the topic of composting narrowly in *Mini Farming: Self Sufficiency on ¼ Acre* by describing its importance and how to make thermophilic aerobic compost. As thermophilic aerobic compost is the standard for organic production, even though I also do other forms of composting, I didn't think other forms would be very interesting to my readers.

My readers quickly disabused me of that notion via email and in person. I receive more "what if . . ." questions about composting than any other topic. After sending off a few dozen multi-page answers on everything from vermicompost to anaerobic digesters, I realized there is a need for far more comprehensive information on compost, and for it to all be readily accessible in one place. In addition, I started encountering avid gardeners who were even more pressed for time than myself or who had physical limitations that would keep them from turning tons of compost. These folks needed solutions to help composting fit into their lives.

So the inspiration for this book can be entirely attributed to my wonderful and thoughtful readers, without whom it would never have been written. My readers also made this book possible in another very important way: by buying my other books, they gave my publisher the confidence to publish this one as well! Publishing books requires a lot of behind-the-scenes work in graphic design and layout plus some pretty heavy up-front costs. I am not a very good sales person and I have never given much thought to how to convince a publisher to undertake the risks and expenses of publishing a book. But my readers have made it so I can just be myself and not have to be an expert in sales in order to get this published.

This book is dedicated to my readers, with humble thanks for both their insight and support. What good is writing if nobody is there to read it?

1

Introduction to Composting

In general, compost can be described as organic matter that has decayed to a point of biological stability, but such a generalized definition doesn't tell us much. The reason generalizations fail is because compost can be made from practically anything that was once alive, and it can be made using a vast array of methods. Every variation produces something different, so no two batches of compost are the same.

Compost can be made both aerobically (using oxygen) and anaerobically (without oxygen). It can be made at relatively high temperatures (thermophilically) or at moderate temperatures (mesophilically). You can even make it using earthworms as digesters. Though doing so is inefficient, it can be made entirely from a single starting ingredient, or from any mixture of ingredients. All of these approaches can be combined at various stages, and each has benefits that are balanced against shortcomings. The potential for confusion can seem insurmountable, which may be why anytime I go somewhere to speak, I get questions about composting.

The happy reality though, is that nature is on your side. It's really hard to mess up compost so badly that you get no compost at all. Nature loves compost and will turn anything that was once alive (or produced by something living) into compost all by itself. Biological materials will naturally degrade, and composting those materials is simply a way of accelerating or controlling the process. Though there are many ways of composting, each with its own trade-offs, nature will ultimately have its way and organic materials will rot with or without your help. The end product will be compost. So the most important thing you need to do when approaching composting is to not worry.

In the chapters ahead I'll take you through the nutrient cycle, explain the role of compost in soil microbiology and plant health, and delve into the various methods of composting. Even though I will stress a lot of points as being important, if you keep coming back to the fundamental concept that *organic materials will all eventually turn into compost with or without your help,* you'll realize that you can just dig right in and your end results will be a tremendous benefit no matter what.

Nearly all books that cover compost concentrate only on aerobic composting with a special emphasis on thermophilic composting. But this is not, in my opinion, enough to make someone self-sufficient. For example, maybe you have noticed that you need compost for soil blocks when you are starting your onion seedlings in January, but your outdoor compost pile is going to be frozen until April so it won't do you any good. Or maybe you have a back or leg injury, and turning a two-ton thermophilic aerobic compost pile is simply not feasible.

Because nature is on your side, there are a lot of different ways to create compost, and all that is really necessary is an underlying understanding of the nature of the processes at work and an eye toward safety to adapt numerous methods to your situation. I personally use many methods both indoors and outdoors, and this book will help you do the same.

Why Use Compost?

If you are looking at this book, you're probably already sold on the idea of composting. If you aren't already sold, then I am going to convince you.

Whether you garden using chemical fertilizers, pesticides and fungicides, or using organic methods, there is abundant and compelling scientific proof that compost will improve the fertility of your soil so that less fertilizer is needed. It will also reduce the incidence and severity of diseases that reduce your crop yield. The math is straightforward: using compost means your garden will be more cost-effective because you will have to spend less money on fertilizers, insecticides, and fungicides for a given harvest of any crop. That means *money*. A lot of money.

Compost induces resistance to a wide array of bacterial and fungal diseases.[1] Induced resistance (as opposed to acquired immunity) is a form of epigenetics. That is, how a plant or animal expresses its genes is not controlled simply by the genes themselves, but also how various environmental factors affect that expression. Plants were not intended to be grown in sterile soil. Rather, they were intended to be grown in living soil. Compost creates and sustains a living soil, so when grown in the proper environment as nature intended, the gene expression of plants is optimized for their health.

This concept also applies to humans. Humans were never intended to be sedentary bumps on a log. Studies show that proper exercise literally turns certain genes on or off and thereby affects our vulnerability to a host of diseases to a substantial degree.[2] So the fact that environmental factors such as the presence of compost can have a large effect on the well-being of plants is not at all surprising. When humans eat right and get their exercise, the aggregate cost of health care is reduced. When plants eat right, the cost of their health care is also reduced. Just as a human in optimal health is more productive, a plant grown in soil amended with compost has greater yields.[3]

1   Vallad, G., Cooperband, L., and Goodman, R., "Plant foliar disease suppression mediated by composted forms of paper mill residuals exhibits molecular forms of induced resistance.", *Physical and Molecular Plant Pathology* 63 (2003): 65–77

2   Agus, D., *The End of Illness*, (New York: Free Press, 2012)

3   Edwards, S. et al., *The Impact of Compost Use on Crop Yields in Tigray, Ethiopia*, 2000-2006 Inclusive, ISBN 978-983-2729-91-4.

According to the Washington State University Cooperative Extension Service (along with dozens of other sources), compost helps soil retain fertilizers better, and also reduces or even eliminates the need for fertilizer altogether. Fertilizer, like fungicides, costs money. WSU also states that the beneficial microorganisms in compost can help protect crops from pests, thereby reducing the need for pesticides. That's even more money.

So right there, if you garden and your intention in gardening is to save money over buying an equivalent product at the grocery store, the case for using compost is open and shut—done. If you aren't using compost, you are throwing money away.

Another reason to use compost is human health. Depending on which experts you ask, humans need anywhere from twenty-two to fifty elements in their diet for optimal health. I am not speaking of vitamins and other complex molecules, but rather basic chemical elements that we need in order to catalyze the synthesis of cellular enzymes or even as core constituents of structures such as bones. Though a person can survive and even thrive for a time with an ongoing deficiency in some of these elements, over time deficiency takes its toll, and some USDA researchers have come to believe that most cancer and as many as 50 percent of all deaths globally are caused directly or indirectly by insufficient intake of important trace elements.[4]

Though this information has not been widely disseminated in an environment where other branches of the

---

4   Banuelos, G., and Lin, Z.(eds), *Development and Uses of Biofortified Agricultural Products* (CRC Press, 2008)

USDA continue to push nutritionally vapid commodities as "healthy", it is available for those who care to search. In fact, long before the USDA researchers came along, Dr. Maynard Murray conducted numerous experiments demonstrating dramatically reduced risks of cancer and many other chronic diseases in animals fed foods grown in such a way as to contain as many elements as possible.[5]

Many find it puzzling that in an era where preventable causes of cancer and heart disease are in decline, many other forms of cancer and heart disease are increasing. But taken with the information above, it might not seem so surprising once we realize that the elemental content of agricultural soil has declined by 85 percent over the past 100 years[6] and the nutritional content of commercially available foods has declined by anywhere from 30 percent to 81 percent over the past thirty years.

So the elements in the soil you use for growing food are important. The full complement of elements is certainly important for the well-being of your crops, and assists them in fending off pests and diseases through their own robust immune systems. But the elements in your soil are also important for the well-being of the people who eat those crops, including you.

Standard agricultural methods can be described as having mined all the nutritionally necessary minerals out of the soil. Those methods return a handful of elements in the form of fertilizer, but only thirteen elements are generally required to grow a good-looking and marketable food commodity in a

5   Murray, M., *Sea Energy Agriculture* (Acres USA, 2003 (reprint))
6   Marler, J. and Wallin, J., Nutritionsecurity.org "Human Health, the Nutritional Quality of Harvested Food and Sustainable Farming Systems"

competitive market that doesn't distinguish one tomato from another. All of the other elements needed for human health—elements that were abundantly present a century ago—are either absent or severely depleted.

Compost contains and preserves these micronutrients that are so important to human health. So if you grow a garden for your health, you really need to use compost otherwise you are largely wasting your time.

Why Make Your Own Compost?

If you weren't already convinced of the value of adding compost to your garden soil, I hope I have convinced you. But the next question is: why should you make compost yourself rather than just buying it?

Cost-effectiveness in a home garden requires different methods than those employed in large commercial farms. Substantially enhanced nutrition and major cost savings can only be achieved in a home garden through the use of sustainable and organic methods,[7] and the primary practice that enables these methods is *composting*.

If you have read *Mini Farming: Self Sufficiency on ¼ Acre*, you know that I put a great deal of emphasis on compost. That emphasis is not misplaced, because composting is the primary method that will help to retain the elemental content of your soil in a biological matrix that will make it available to plants as needed, without being washed out of your soil.

---

7   My books *Mini Farming: Self Sufficiency on ¼ Acre* and *Mini Farming: Maximizing Your Mini Farm* cover cost-effective and sustainable methods.

Keep in mind that there is no such thing as a perfectly sustainable system because, if you eat the food you grow, part of that mineral content is retained in your body and some is discarded as waste. But even then, the mineral conservation achieved through composting substantially reduces the amount of minerals you will need to supply via outside sources.

Likewise, for a variety of reasons, few soils available to homeowners and renters already contain an optimum mineral content, and they will need to be supplemented with the required minerals. But once those minerals are in the soil, conscientious composting practices will help to retain them, so that fewer will need to be added in the future.

Fewer additives equates to less money being spent for the value of the produce you raise. So composting will allow you to raise more sturdy plants that provide superior nutrition for less money. If self-sufficiency or health are your objectives, composting is not optional—it's necessary.

Though you may need to buy bagged compost when you start gardening, bagged compost is extremely expensive. Though it varies from crop to crop, in general you may need to add anywhere from two to eight cubic feet of compost for every thirty-two square feet of garden. At the time of writing, bagged compost costs anywhere from $5 to $8 per cubic foot. It wouldn't take a very big garden for this to run into hundreds or even thousands of dollars. And what you get for all that money may not be what you expect.

When you buy bagged commercial compost, you have no idea what went into it. Though the regulations for USDA Certified Organic agriculture prohibit the use of sewage sludge on crops labeled as "USDA Organic", there is no such prohibition on the labeling of bagged compost, and many types of compost labeled as "organic" contain sewage sludge.[8]

In theory, composting human waste is just fine, provided it is done in a fashion that eliminates pathogens. Even drug metabolites in human waste are often effectively destroyed or rendered biologically inert as part of the composting process. But sewage sludge is *not* a result of such a composting process, and large-scale waste treatment systems are not equipped to remove many harmful chemicals. Humans consume a vast array of chemicals in the form of medications, artificial colors, preservatives and so forth. The levels of drug metabolites in our waste stream are so high that pharmaceuticals such as Prozac have shown up in water supplies.[9] Sewage sludge also contains more than merely human waste. Sludge contains the chemicals, hair dyes, heavy metals, paint, degreasers, detergents and motor oil people wash down their drains, drugs that are not detoxified by the sewage treatment process and more. An EPA survey of sludge samples conducted in 2009 found detectable levels of a dozen drugs, flame retardants and even endocrine disruptors.

So if you DO wind up buying bagged compost, please pay attention to the fine print and ask about its contents.

As previously stated, bagged compost is pretty expensive. If when you start your garden you have to buy compost because you have made none of your own, it will be more cost-effective to have it delivered by the truckload if such an option exists

---

8   Arnell, N., "Many types of organic compost are really packaged human sewage", Natural News.com, May 6 2011
9   Townsend, M., "Stay Calm Everyone, There's Prozac in the Drinking Water", *The Observer*, 7 August 2004

for you. Compost delivered by truck is measured in yards. As a point of reference, a yard of compost is twenty-seven cubic feet. I have had compost delivered on a couple of occasions. In both cases the compost was not yet finished and couldn't be used until the next season. In one instance the compost contained asphalt rocks and even hypodermic syringes. (Yikes!)

So remember, just as food you grow yourself is superior because it is grown with your own well-being as a priority, so is compost that you make yourself. *It is in your best interests to start making your own compost* because it is far less expensive and because you control its ingredients and how it is made.

Making your own compost is easy, and I have written this book to show you how.

2

Starting with the Soil

Though this book is about composting, compost is intended to conserve or augment the soil in your garden. As the nutrient cycle starts with your garden soil, and any nutrients conserved through composting started out in the soil of your garden, a comprehensive examination of your soil and the ways it might be improved is a good place to start.

As a gardener you want soil that will hold adequate moisture without becoming so waterlogged as to exclude oxygen from the roots. You also want soil rich in organic matter that will hold nutrients and release them to the roots as needed. Soil should also be within the ideal pH range of most plants you'll grow, and your soil should have adequate levels of the nutrients plants need most, such as nitrogen, phosphorus, and potassium. Ideally, you want soil that doesn't crust over so seeds can sprout. Finally, you want soil with a broad spectrum of micro-nutrients both for the optimum health of the plants and the health of those who eat them.

In practice, few gardeners start with such ideal soil. Soil either has too much sand, too much clay, too high or low a pH, or lacks fundamental nutrients including nitrogen, phosphorus and potassium. To say that the soil most homeowners have to work with is less than ideal would be an understatement, considering that in many cases their yards are composed of sand and filled with only enough loam to start grass. Just under the grass mat what passes for soil looks awfully sterile. How do you start the rehabilitation process?

Analyzing Your Soil's Water Characteristics

Soil has three important characteristics pertaining to water: infiltration, percolation and available water-holding capacity.

Infiltration is a measure of how quickly water is absorbed into the soil. Quicker infiltration means less water is either lost or runs off. Percolation is how quickly water that is in excess of what the soil can hold leaves the soil. Available water-holding capacity is how much water the soil can hold. In practice, if you can get the infiltration and percolation rates within reasonable ranges, your water holding capacity will take care of itself.

Analyze percolation rate by digging a hole 1' deep and 6"–8" in diameter, and keep it topped off with water for at least four hours on the day before you test. The day you test, adjust the water level in the hole to 6" from the bottom (use a plastic ruler). Next, set a timer for ten minutes. At the end of ten minutes, use a ruler to measure how many inches the water fell. Bring the water level back up to 6", repeat the process, and average the two distances. The percolation rate in minutes per inch (MPI) is: MPI = 10/Distance. You want an MPI of between 60 and 30. If it is greater than 30, use raised beds to prevent waterlogging. If it is less than 6, increase the level of compost you would add based on biological activity by 50 percent. Do this with each compost addition until you have an MPI of 6 or greater.

Infiltration rate is tested two days after a thorough (e.g. equivalent to 1" of rain) watering. It is measured using a "double ring infiltrometer". This fancy sounding gadget is two pieces of PVC pipe, each 8" long, one being 4" in diameter and the other being 6" in diameter. Use a rubber mallet to drive the larger ring 2"–3" deep into the soil, and then drive the smaller ring the same depth in, as close to the middle of the larger ring as is practicable. Fill both the inner and outer rings with water to a 4" or 5" depth. (Use a ruler.) Now, set your timer for ten minutes. At the end of ten minutes, measure how much the water level has decreased in the center tube. Refill both rings and repeat twice more, then average your results. Your infiltration rate is: Infiltration = 10/Distance. If your infiltration rate is less than 2, your soil is too sandy and you can help with compost or by adding the same amount of peat

⊗ Testing the soil's percolation rate.

moss as you would compost. If your infiltration rate is greater than 10, your soil likely has too much clay. Add gypsum with your other soil amendments at the rate of 10 lb per 100 sq. ft. Test annually, and continue to add gypsum with your other amendments until the infiltration rate is greater than 10.

While it is recommended that gardens be watered at a rate that approximates 1" of rain weekly,[10] the amount and frequency of watering is determined to some degree by soil variables. Though these can be tested, it is far easier to just observe. Start off by checking to see if your crops look like

---

10 I explain how to do this with a standard watering attachment, bucket and timer in *Mini Farming: Self Sufficiency on ¼ Acre*.

they need water in less than a week. If they do, then you know you should be watering more often. Watering more in a given session likely will not help because the excess water will simply drain, but watering more frequently will supply what is needed. Over time, additions of compost will improve water-holding capacity. If the water-holding capacity seems seriously lacking, you can amend with vermiculite at the rate of two cubic feet of vermiculite per thirty-two square feet of garden soil. Vermiculite is mica that has been heated and popped like popcorn, and it does well at taking up and releasing water.

Analyzing Your Soil's Biological Activity

A very important factor that should be measured in soil is its biological activity. This is the quantity and activity of microorganisms in the soil. The health of microbes in the soil is important because it is the interaction between microbes and the roots of plants that converts nutrients from an organic form useless to the plants into an inorganic form that plants can readily assimilate. Such a measurement reflects many underlying factors of soil fertility, as healthy microbes indicate a healthy soil. Furthermore, microbes tie up certain nutrients and make them available as needed. Thus, the amount of supplementation for nitrogen that a soil test indicates is required can be reduced if biological activity is high. This is because a soil test for nitrogen only tests for inorganic nitrates, and can't take the nitrogen available in microorganisms into account. Likewise, the biological activity of a soil can be used to determine how much compost needs to be added.

There are two ways to measure the biological activity of soil: respiration testing, and counting the number of earthworms. Both methods are best used in mid-spring or mid-fall because either extremely hot or extremely cold weather will falsely suppress the results. The earthworm method is the easiest: a couple of days after a good rain, using a flat spade, dig up a 1' × 1' × 1' cube of soil from your garden, dump it into a wheelbarrow or onto a flat piece of wood and count the earthworms.

Earthworm testing is the easiest (and least expensive) method available, but there are some areas where the soil is perfectly fine but earthworms have simply never been

⊗ Counting earthworms is the easiest and least expensive method of assessing your soil's biological activity.

introduced[11] or don't thrive for some other reason. In those cases, soil biological activity can be measured via respiration testing, which measures the amount of carbon dioxide generated by microbes in the soil.

Because respiration testing is expensive, I have searched for cheaper methods. The problem is that the amount of carbon dioxide generated by a practical amount of soil is measured in millionths of a gram, so such methods aren't practical for home use.

One method would be to make a liter of saturated lime water solution, and inject the air trapped over a section of soil into the lime water. (Lime water is 1.5 g of calcium hydroxide dissolved in a liter of distilled water.) As carbon dioxide combined with the calcium hydroxide to form calcium carbonate, the calcium carbonate would precipitate out of solution. It could be caught on filter paper and weighed. The weight of the calcium carbonate could then be used to determine how much carbon dioxide had been captured. The trouble is that the amount of calcium carbonate created would be so small that weighing it would not be practical on scales that are generally affordable. This problem could possibly be solved by collecting air over a fairly large area (e.g. a square yard), but this becomes logistically difficult.

The two generally available methods that will accurately measure such small quantities of carbon dioxide are the Solvita Basic Soil Respiration Test ($120 for material to perform six tests) and the USDA Soil Quality Test Kit, which costs over

---

11 Earthworms became extinct in North America during the past couple of Ice Ages and were re-introduced by European explorers.

$800 from Gempler's in Iowa. Thankfully, you can use only a subset of the latter kit in order to perform the soil respiration test. Even so, the initial cost will be somewhat high, but ongoing costs (i.e. a new Draeger™ tube for each test at $6.50 each) will be more reasonable in the long run. Again, let me point out that if you can count earthworms in your soil, this isn't needed.

Biological Activity Measurement
Materials Needed

- 1 × 6" diameter piece of 1/8" thick aluminum pipe 5" long, a clearly scribed line should be marked 2" from one end and the edge of the other end should be beveled—contact a local welding shop.
- 1 × 6" stove-pipe cap, with two 1/2" holes drilled in it. The holes should be 1" from the edges, opposite each other.
- 2 × #00 rubber stoppers
- 8" long piece of 2"−4" lumber
- 2−4 lb rubber mallet or mini sledgehammer
- Soil thermometer
- 2" × 6" long sections of latex tubing, 3/16" outside diameter, 1/8" inside diameter
- 2 × 18 to 22 gauge 1.5" hypodermic needles
- 140 cc syringe
- Pack of 10 × Draeger tubes, 0.1% CO_2
- Timer that will time up to 30 minutes

Procedure

- The day before you plan to conduct the test, water the soil thoroughly, to the equivalent of 1" of rain.

- Place the beveled edge of the pipe against the dirt. Lay the 8" long board across the pipe, and use the mallet or hammer to bang the pipe into the dirt until it is level with the inscribed line.
- Cover the pipe with the lid and wait for 30 minutes. If the lid doesn't form an airtight seal, use some duct tape to tape the bottom edge of the lid to the pipe.
- While you are waiting, insert the soil thermometer 2"−3" into the soil immediately adjacent to the pipe.
- Also while you are waiting, assemble the measurement apparatus as follows:
  - Use nail clippers to break the nipples off both ends of a Draeger tube.
  - Note that the tube has an arrow indicating direction of airflow.
  - Make sure the syringe piston is fully depressed, and connect a piece of tubing from the syringe to the end of the Draeger tube where the arrow is pointing.
  - Connect the other piece of tubing on the opposite end of the Draeger tube, and attach one of the needles to the far end of the tubing.
- After 30 minutes, insert the needle in the measurement apparatus through one of the stoppers into the head space inside the pipe, and insert the other needle (which is attached to nothing) through the other stopper to provide for airflow. Draw air through the Draeger tube by pulling back slowly on the plunger at the rate of 5 cc per second until 100 cc of air has been drawn into the syringe.
- Read the color change on the Draeger tube. If the color change has not reached the 0.5 mark in the column labeled

"n = 1", take 4 additional samples. Expel the air from the syringe before each sample by first disconnecting it from the tubing and then reconnecting it to the tubing before the next draw. Do all 5 draws at the rate of 5 cc per second until 100 cc of air has been drawn into the syringe. Read the results from the "n = 5" column on the Draeger tube.

You can calculate the amount of CO_2 (and hence the soil respiration and its biological activity) through use of the following formula:

T = Soil temperature in degrees Celsius. If your thermometer reads in Fahrenheit you can convert from Fahrenheit to Celsius:

$$Celsius = \frac{5 \times (Fahrenheit - 32)}{9}$$

P = Percent CO_2 as reported in the appropriate column on the Draeger tube

Grams of CO_2 − C per Square meter per Day
$$= ((T - 273)/273) \times (P - 0.035) \times 10.4$$

Amount of Compost to Add Based on Measurements				
Earthworms per Cubic Foot	Grams CO_2/ m^2/Day	Solvita Test Result #	Cubic Feet of Compost to Add per 32 ft²	Biology Level
20 or more	2.9 or more	3.5+	1.5	A
10–19	1.4–2.9	2.5–3.5	1.5–2.5	B
5–10	0.85–1.4	1.0–2.5	2.5–3.5	C
<5	<0.85	<1.0	3.5–5.5	D

Analyzing Macro-nutrients and pH

If you have ever seen a series of numbers on a bag of fertilizer, such as 10-10-10, 5-10-5 or even 45-0-0, those numbers are the NPK rating of the fertilizer. They mean that 100 lbs of that fertilizer will supply the stated number of pounds of nitrogen, phosphorus or potassium. So 100 lbs of 5-10-5 fertilizer will provide 5 lbs of nitrogen, 10 lbs of phosphorus and 5 lbs of potassium. Because other macro-nutrients such as calcium, carbon and water are supplied as part of liming, watering or simply from the air, these three major nutrients are the ones described on the bag.

Depending upon the type of fertilizer, the rest of the product may be utterly inert, or it may contain other nutrients as well.

Soil analysis is a very complex field and there are two major competing schools of thought regarding what is important. The sufficiency method is used by most laboratories and commercial farms. It tests for the major macro-nutrients: nitrogen, phosphorus and potassium, along with pH and a handful of micro-nutrients The analysis is accompanied by recommendations for additions. You can test the first four of these yourself using home testing kits available at home and garden stores.

The Albrecht method measures the amounts and ratios of positively charged bases (such as calcium, magnesium, potassium, sodium, ammonium and several trace minerals) in the soil. Albrecht's base saturation theory then recommends amendments in proportions that will both raise the saturation level of bases as needed and adjust their relative proportions for optimum conservation of organic matter and soil fertility. The only comparative study undertaken to date, however, concludes that using the Albrecht method gives no significant improvement in crop yield, but costs more.[12]

⊗ Readily available soil testing kits are entirely sufficient for the home gardener's needs.

I therefore recommend the sufficiency method, which has the added bonus of also being something you can do yourself with at-home soil testing kits. Though I use the LaMotte Soil Testing Kit, the other commonly available kits (such as Rapitest) work just as well so long as you follow the directions precisely and use bottled water (rather than tap water) for mixing with the soil. (A lot of tap water has a substantially "off" pH. My uncorrected tap water, for example, has a pH of 4.8, which is low enough to alter soil test results.)

When you gather soil for a soil test, clear the top inch of soil away and then gather your sample. Do this in several places, collecting a heaping tablespoon from each location. Mix them all together in a jar. I happen to use raised bed gardening, so I test each bed, gathering my sample from several places within each bed. If you are using a tilled plot, just gather from several sites in the plot if the soil is reasonably uniform. If the soil is obviously variable within the plot, test the different areas separately.

---

12 Exner, Rick, "Soil Fertility Management Strategies – Philosophies, Crop Response, and Costs" (Iowa State University, University Extension, 2007)

Each soil test has its own instructions which will vary with manufacturer, so I'll leave you to perform the tests. As the tests rely on comparing the color of a solution to the color of a chart, the one piece of advice I would give is to view the tests in the shade on a sunny day as that will give the most true color comparison. If you can't do that, fluorescent lighting is your next best bet. I put a sheet of white paper behind my solution and color comparison chart to aid in interpreting the colors.

Interpreting Soil Test Results

Except for pH, the results of home soil tests are not given in absolute numbers. Instead, they are reported broadly as "depleted", "deficient", "adequate", or "sufficient". If the test indicates sufficient levels of a nutrient, then nothing need be added, but if the test indicates anything less than sufficiency you'll need to supplement the soil.

The reason why I detailed testing biological activity before discussing analysis of macro-nutrients is because, with regard to nitrogen, the amount of nitrogen you need to add is modified depending upon the amount of biological activity. DNA and other proteins present in soil microbes contain nitrogen that will be made available to plants throughout the course of the season, but won't show up in a soil test because a soil test only shows inorganic nitrogen. The amount of nitrogen to be added according to soil test assumes a certain level of biological activity, but if your level of biological activity is greater than the assumed level, you should add less nitrogen than the test recommends. Conversely, if your biological activity is less than the assumed level, you should add more nitrogen than the test recommends.

In general, I recommend using at least two sources of a given macro-nutrient. This will distribute a greater variety of accompanying micro-nutrients and because the sources will break down at different rates, they will provide nutrient availability throughout the season. The following tables show the amount of a given organic fertilizer to use given a certain soil test result. In the case of nitrogen, the table takes biological activity into account. Because the amount of nitrogen needed is lower for root crops, the results are shown with a slash between them, with leaf and fruit crops as the first number and root crops as the second number.

Nitrogen Needed in Ounces per 100 ft²			
	Depleted	Deficient	Adequate
Biology Level A	3 leaf/2 root	1.5 leaf/1 root	1 leaf/0.5 root
Biology Level B	4.5 leaf/3 root	3 leaf/2 root	1.5 leaf/1 root
Biology Level C	6 leaf/4 root	4.5 leaf/3 root	3 leaf/2 root
Biology Level D	7.5 leaf/5 root	6 leaf/4 root	4.5 leaf/3 root

Phosphorus Needed in Ounces per 100 ft²			
	Depleted	Deficient	Adequate
Phosphorus Required	5 ounces	3 ounces	1.25 ounces

Potassium Needed in Ounces per 100 ft²			
	Depleted	Deficient	Adequate
Potassium Required	5.5 ounces	3.5 ounces	1.5 ounces

Compounding Your Own Fertilizer

The foregoing numbers are interesting, but not very useful by themselves because you can't go down to the store and buy five ounces of phosphorus or three ounces of potassium. In fact, in their pure forms, phosphorus is poisonous and incendiary and potassium will explode on contact with moisture. Instead, you'll need to figure out a mix of natural substances that will give you what you need. I have never found a book or website that goes beyond listing the NPK values of various natural substances and actually teaches you how to combine them to get what you need. All it takes is a little math, which, in an era of scientific calculators and computerized spreadsheets, isn't really a problem. First, here is a table listing the NPK values of various substances used as natural fertilizers. Keep in mind that this table is an average

NPK Values of Common Organic Nutrient Sources

	Nitrogen	Phosphorus	Potassium
Substances in Which Nitrogen Predominates			
Alfalfa meal	3	1	2
Soybean meal	2.5	0	2
Dried blood	12	3	0
Cottonseed meal	7	2.5	2
Bat guano	11	2	2
Substances in Which Phosphorus Predominates			
Bone meal	2	21	0
Rock phosphate	0	39	0
Seabird guano	11	11	2
Substances in Which Potassium Predominates			
Wood ashes	0	1.5	8
Greensand	0	1.5	7
Seaweed, dried	1.3	1	5
Kelp meal	1	0	2

of various brands, whose composition varies. If you buy a bag of bone meal and it lists different numbers, use those numbers instead of those in the table. The table is most useful for things that don't usually have numbers – such as wood ashes or alfalfa meal.

There is an easy way to use the tables in this section to make fertilizer, and it is entirely close enough that your plants won't know the difference. There is also a more difficult way that gives you very tight accuracy, which I'll explain after I've demonstrated the easy way.

I will demonstrate the easy way with an example. Pretend you have tested your garden soil, found it is biology class B, has deficient nitrogen, adequate phosphorus and deficient potassium. You will be growing a root crop. Looking at the tables, this means that you need to create a fertilizer that provides 2 oz. of nitrogen, 1.25 oz. of phosphorus and 3.5 oz. of potassium per 100 sq. ft.

The equations for the number of ounces of an organic source you need in order to get a certain number of ounces of nutrient are:

Nitrogen Source Ounces = 100 × (Nitrogen Ounces Needed/"N" Value from Table)

Phosphorus Source Ounces = 100 × (Phosphorus Ounces Needed/"P" Value from Table)

Potassium Source Ounces = 100 × (Potassium Ounces Needed/"K" Value from Table)

The table of organic nutrient sources is divided into three sections according to which nutrient predominates. Pick whatever you have or can readily acquire from each category. For example, I will pick soybean meal for nitrogen, bone meal for phosphorus and greensand for potassium.

The N number for soybean meal is 2.5 and I need 2 oz. of nitrogen, so:

$$\text{Ounces of Soybean Meal Needed} = 100 \times (2/2.5)$$
$$= 80 \text{ oz.}$$

The P number for bone meal is 21, and I need 1.25 oz. of phosphorus, so:

$$\text{Ounces of Bone Meal Needed} = 100 \times (1.25/21)$$
$$= 6 \text{ oz.}$$

The K number for greensand is 7 and I need 3.5 oz. of potassium, so:

$$\text{Ounces of Greensand Needed} = 100 \times (3.5/7)$$
$$= 50 \text{ oz.}$$

Based upon these calculations, in order to make a complete fertilizer for 100 sq. ft, I need to combine 50 oz. of greensand with 28 oz. of soybean meal and 6 oz. of bone meal.

This fertilizer is a bit off from precisely what you need, because soybean meal also contains a substantial amount of potassium, and bone meal also contains some nitrogen. In practice, this isn't a problem because the ingredients, being organic, aren't instantly available to plants so a bit of an over-abundance won't hurt as much as it would if you were using chemicals such as ammonium nitrate as fertilizer.

But if you were to use alfalfa meal and dried seaweed as ingredients, keep in mind that they contain almost as much of one nutrient as another, so using the easy technique could lead to an overabundance of fertilizer. Though it might not be an immediate problem, over the course of a season an over-abundance of some nutrients (such as nitrogen) can lead to undesirable outcomes such as plants making all vegetation and no fruits or tubers. Other nutrients in excess can block the absorption of micro-nutrients. So a little bit of over-fertilization is okay, but you don't want to go too far. If you are using fertilizer components that contain substantial amounts of more than one nutrient, then you'll be better off using the more difficult method.

The solution is to use algebra to solve a system of equations. The number of equations and variables is the same as the number of ingredients. For a fertilizer composed of three ingredients, the equations would be:

$$(F_1 \times n_1/100) + (F_2 \times n_2/100) + (F_3 \times n_3/100) = N$$
$$(F_1 \times p_1/100) + (F_2 \times p_2/100) + (F_3 \times p_3/100) = P$$
$$(F_1 \times k_1/100) + (F_2 \times k_2/100) + (F_3 \times k_3/100) = K$$

Where:

F_1 = Ounces of the first fertilizer (this is unknown)
n_1, p_1, k_1 = The NPK values for that fertilizer from the table (or the bag)

F_2 = Ounces of the second fertilizer (this is unknown)

n_2, p_2, k_2 = The NPK values for that fertilizer from the table (or the bag)

F_3 = Ounces of the third fertilizer (this is unknown)

n_3, p_3, k_3 = The NPK values for that fertilizer from the table (or the bag)

N = Ounces of nitrogen needed per 100 sq. ft

P = Ounces of phosphorus needed per 100 sq. ft

K = Ounces of potassium needed per 100 sq. ft

This looks far more complicated than it really is. Repeating the prior example, using a combination of soybean meal (fertilizer 1), bone meal (fertilizer 2), and greensand (fertilizer 3) to provide 2 oz. of nitrogen, 1.25 oz. of phosphorus and 3.5 oz. of potassium, the equations look like this:

$$(F_1 \times 2.5/100) + (F_2 \times 2/100) + (F_3 \times 0/100) = 2$$
$$(F_1 \times 0/100) + (F_2 \times 21/100) + (F_3 \times 1.5/100) = 1.25$$
$$(F_1 \times 2/100) + (F_2 \times 0/100) + (F_3 \times 7/100) = 3.5$$

The system of equations can be solved via the substitution method or using matrices and determinants. Or, because we live in a wonderful age, you can literally type the equations right into a web site and it will solve them for you. The website www.solvemymath.com has such a calculator at the time of writing, but there are several others that show up via Internet searches.

Solving the system of equations shows that, for every 100 sq. ft, 77 oz. of soybean meal, 4 oz. of bone meal and 28 oz. of greensand would be needed to provide the necessary elements. These numbers differ from those obtained using the easy approach because they take into account the fact that most organic fertilizers supply more than one nutrient. If the solution to the system of equations gives you a negative number for the amount of one of the ingredients, then come up with a different set of ingredients because that combination won't work.

Using these methods will allow you to mix a custom combined fertilizer to meet any likely need for nutrient augmentation.

Micro-nutrients

Micro-nutrients can be broadly divided into two categories: those needed for the optimal health of crops and those needed for the optimal health of humans. The latter category is much broader and, depending upon which expert is consulted, can include as many as fifty elements, whereas only thirteen are needed for plants to look marketable. The categories overlap, so supplying the elements needed for humans would include those needed for plants.

I advocate a three-tier approach to micro-nutrients The first tier is to use compost, and to add other soil amendments from a variety of sources so that many micro-nutrients are naturally present and conserved. The second tier is to specifically add micro-nutrients that are generally required by plants. The third tier is to include a small quantity of a broad spectrum micro-nutrient additive that will include everything humans need so it is available for uptake by the crops.

The micro-nutrients generally required by plants are boron, copper, iron, magnesium, manganese, molybdenum, sulfur, and zinc.

Boron: Boron is critical to practically all life processes in a plant, ranging from regulation of water uptake to the generation of hormones. You can add boron in the form of borax (from the cleaning aisle at the supermarket). You need three teaspoons per 100 square feet of garden annually. Boron is toxic to plants in excess, so don't exceed the recommended amount. Boron deficiency gives different symptoms depending on the plant. In general, root crops suffering from boron deficiency develop tubers that either have hollow cores or cores that are very prone to rotting. In vegetable crops, you may find hollow or roughened stems, stunted growth, and yellow tips on the leaves.

Copper: Copper is important for root metabolism, photosynthesis and enzyme activation. It is only needed in small amounts, and excess amounts can kill plants, so don't exceed the recommended amount. If you use copper-based fungicides, you don't need to add it as a micro-nutrient because you already have at least enough and probably too much in your soil. I recommend adding copper in the form of copper sulfate crystals. These are bright blue and unmistakable. Use four tablespoons per 100 square feet of garden annually. Suspect copper deficiency if newer leaves are wilted and older leaves have a pronounced tendency to curl inward on themselves.

Iron: Iron is crucial for the chlorophyll cycle in plants. Without it, they will take on a bleached-out appearance and their growth will be stunted. Plants self-regulate their iron uptake, so a slightly excess amount won't hurt anything. If, like me, you use blood meal in your garden, iron deficiency isn't an issue. But if you don't use blood meal, you can add iron in the form of iron (ferrous) sulfate. I recommend six ounces per 100 square feet of garden.

Magnesium: Magnesium's primary benefit is that it helps your soil bacteria, but it also plays a role in carbohydrate motility within the plants. Magnesium coexists naturally in dolomitic lime. If you substitute a portion of dolomitic lime with regular lime in your garden, you don't need to supplement magnesium. If you don't use dolomitic lime, you can get magnesium sulfate (a.k.a. Epsom salt) at the grocery store and add it to your garden at the rate of between twelve and twenty-four ounces per 100 square feet annually. Magnesium deficiency will cause the spaces between the veins of the leaves to look bleached-out at first, and then some of the tissue will die and turn brown. In brassicas, the bleached-out areas may include other pigments such as orange or violet.

Manganese: Manganese is necessary for photosynthesis and improves the yield of root crops. It is very rare to need manganese unless your soil pH is naturally higher than 6.5, which is also rare. Soils that are over-farmed can be deficient, but this is unlikely to apply to your garden. If manganese deficiency symptoms occur anyway, as manifested in a uniform yellowing of *new* leaves,[13] you can add manganese sulfate at the rate of twelve ounces per 100 square feet. Only add this once every three years as it tends to remain in the soil. Slight manganese deficiency is hard to spot because it looks like an extremely mild case of iron deficiency. In more severe cases, leaves develop a definite grayish metallic sheen and spots of dead tissue appear along the veins.

Molybdenum: Molybdenum is needed for practically every cellular process in a plant. Most soils are deficient in molybdenum. In excess, it is extremely toxic to plants. Fur-

---

13 Yellowing of *old* leaves is a sign of nitrogen deficiency.

thermore, a slight excess of molybdenum will exacerbate any existing problems with manganese deficiency. Sufficient levels of copper will mitigate the adverse effects from an excess of molybdenum. For this reason, I recommend that if molybdenum is added, it should be added in conjunction with copper and manganese. If you add molybdenum, I recommend using sodium molybdate or ammonium molybdate. Ammonium molybdate or sodium molbdate should be added at the rate of one-and-a-half ounces per 100 square feet. Molybdenum deficiency looks like nitrogen deficiency, except the underside of the leaves doesn't look red as they usually will with nitrogen deficiency. (This is because plants need molybdenum to process nitrogen.) In severe cases, leaves will also cup upwards and develop spots of dead tissue.

Sulfur: Sulfur is a component of the amino acids that make the DNA, proteins and enzymes within a plant, and it is therefore critical. Any compound that includes the phrase "sulfate" contains sulfur. So when you add magnesium sulfate (Epsom salt), copper sulfate or calcium sulfate (gypsum) to your soil, you are adding sulfur along with the primary desired nutrient. Sulfur is usually added in the form of plain elemental sulfur, known as flowers of sulfur, at the rate of twenty-four ounces per 100 square feet annually. It tends to lower the pH, so adding it with an equal amount of lime is prudent. Sulfur deficiency shows itself as an overall chlorosis with a distinct pinkness in the veins of the leaves.

Zinc: Zinc is key for seed production and regulation of water equilibrium in plants. It is rare for soils to be deficient in zinc, but if they are deficient it will show up as chlorotic bands within the leaves of plants. The pH of the soil affects how available zinc is to plants. A soil could have plenty of zinc, but still give symptoms of deficiency in alkaline (pH greater than 7) soils. So I would recommend getting the pH down to 6.5 before supplementing zinc. When needed, zinc is used in the form of zinc sulfate at the rate of twelve ounces per 100 square feet annually. A deficiency in zinc manifests in yellowed younger leaves that also show pitting between the veins. Continued deficiency results in the tissues between the veins dying while the veins remain green.

That takes care of the needs of the plants, but what about the nutritional needs of people? What I use and recommend is evaporated ocean water. Such a product is usually called "sea solids", "ocean minerals" or "sea mineral solids".

⊗ Common sources of trace elements include wood ashes, sea solids and borax.

Over the ages, rain and erosion have moved a great many minerals that would ordinarily be on land in abundance into the sea. Over-farming without replenishment and farming practices that lose topsoil to erosion have exacerbated this problem. Though I am able to go to the seashore and collect kelp from the beach for my own compost, this is seldom practical for most people.

In essence, sea water contains, in varying amounts, every known element save those made artificially in nuclear reactors. In 1976, Dr. Maynard Murray published a book entitled *Sea Energy Agriculture* in which he highlighted the results of numerous studies he had made from the 1930s through 1950s on the addition of ocean minerals to agricultural land. Though his book was published some time ago, I have discovered that in growing beds side by side, those treated with sea minerals do, in fact, produce obviously healthier plants.

The big problem with using ocean water directly is obvious: it's really heavy and you can't grow plants in salt water because it kills them. In fact, one of the practices of ancient warfare was to sow your enemies' fields with salt so they wouldn't be fertile. Fortunately, only a small quantity of sea solids is required, and when package directions are followed not only is there no harm, but plants become more healthy and more resistant to insects and diseases. The process is also cost effective as, on a mini farm, the amount of sea minerals required is tiny; so even a ten-pound bag of sea minerals from various sources will literally last for years. (I use five pounds annually when I haven't been able to supplement my compost with seaweed.) There are a number of companies offering sea minerals such as GroPal, Sea Agri, Sea Minerals from Arkansas and others. The key is that each offering is a bit different, so be sure to scale the package directions appropriately.

Do not use "sea salt" in place of these products. Why not? Because most sea salt sold for culinary use is this beautiful crystalline white stuff from which all of the valuable trace nutrients have been removed. There are a few unrefined offerings of culinary sea salt out there, such as Celtic Sea Salt, but these are very expensive for agricultural use.

Now before I go further, I want to discuss the effect of composting on micro-nutrients. In all likelihood, your soil will start off with some degree of deficiency. But when you add nutrients to your soil, they will end up in your plant materials. Then, when you compost the materials and add them back to the soil, the elements will have been conserved. Furthermore, the humic acid will chelate and microorganisms in compost will hold these nutrients, whether the compost is in the pile or has been added to your soil. If you use biochar, that will help the minerals stay in the soil as well.

In commercial agriculture, these elements are often an annual addition. That is because extensive tillage depletes organic matter in the soil, and composting is not usually done on a sufficient scale or with a diversity of ingredients. Thus, the soil doesn't have sufficient ability to hold onto the micro-nutrients and they are washed out with rain, or shipped away with the crops.

If, on the other hand, you are managing your soil fertility with cover crops, crop rotation, using organic soil amend-ments and diligent composting plus even adding some biochar, micro-nutrients will have a greater tendency to stay in your soil. This means that you should not add micro-nutrients annually once your garden is established and compost operations are underway. With the exception of molybdenum which should only be added once, add the other micro-nutrients as recom-mended for the first three years. But after that, you can do just fine by adding ocean minerals every other year, and the only individual micro-nutrient you'll need to add annually is boron.

When adding micro-nutrients, thoroughly mix them with some other amendment that you will add in larger quantities. It is essentially impossible to evenly distribute an ounce and a half of some powder over a 100 square foot area. So these nutrients should be added to materials such as wood ashes or bone meal that are used in larger quantities, thoroughly mixed, and added. That way, and especially for nutrients that could be toxic such as boron, copper or molybdenum, you don't end up with "hot spots" in your garden that won't grow anything.

I have received a number of emails asking where to get these substances, so I am going to give you some sources with the understanding that none of these companies has paid me, that I don't know anyone who works for them personally, and that my listing of them as a source doesn't mean I endorse or even know everything about their political positions, business practices or anything else.

Epsom salt (magnesium sulfate) and borax (sodium tetraborate) are available at any grocery store. Copper sulfate is a common agricultural chemical and should be available at any comprehensive "feed and seed" or agricultural store, as should flowers of sulfur. Iron sulfate is also a common chemical and if you can't find it at your local feed and seed store, you can find it ubiquitously on the Internet via a search for it. I got mine at Kmart, a national department store chain.

Manganese sulfate is also an agricultural chemical, but harder to find via local sources. I ordered mine from Star Nursery (www.starnursery.com) because they sold five pound bags, but there are a lot of other sources. Sodium molybdate is pretty expensive, at over $20 for eight ounces at www.customhydronutrients.com. This is a much better deal than the reagent grade material from a chemical company which will run you $200 to $300 for a similar quantity.

pH

pH is a measure of how acidic or alkaline the soil is. It is important because plants generally have a certain range of pH preference for optimal growth and because the pH of the soil actively affects which microorganisms will thrive in the environment and how readily the nutrients contained in the soil can be used by plants. pH is measured on a scale from 0 to 14. 0 is highly acidic, like battery acid; 14 is highly basic like lye, and 7 is neutral.

Many sources list a pH preference range for each plant, but these sources often differ in the details. For example, one source will list the preferred pH for tomatoes as 5.8 to 6.5, whereas another will list it as 6 to 7. The simple fact is that you don't need to be that detailed because most plants grown for food in gardens will grow well with a pH ranging from 6 to 7. True, a cucumber can grow at a pH as high as 8, but it will also grow at 6.5.

pH corrections can take months to show results and the constant rotation of beds between crops makes it impractical to customize the pH of a bed to a given crop. It therefore makes sense to test each bed individually, and correct the beds to a uniform pH of between 6 and 6.5. The exceptions are that the beds used for potatoes should have the pH lower than 6.5, and the beds used for brassicas (such as cabbage) should have extra lime added to the holes where the transplants are placed.[14]

The cost of pH meters for home use has dropped considerably in recent years, with accurate units selling for as little as $13. Simply follow the directions that come with your individual meter for measuring each bed. You don't need a pH meter, however, because the soil testing kits you use for measuring macro-nutrients also have a test for pH. (The pH meter used for testing soil is not the same type of meter used when testing the pH of beer wort.)

In most of the U.S. the soil pH is too low and needs to be raised to be within an optimal range. Correcting pH using

---

14 This practice prevents the appearance of a disease called "club-foot".

lime can be problematic in that it takes several months to act. Though the gardening year should start in the fall along with any soil corrections, the reality of life is that the decision to start a garden is generally made in the late winter or early spring. Thus, the farmer is stuck trying to correct pH within weeks of planting instead of months.

However, with a bit of creativity and use of alternate materials, both short and long term corrections can be made to pH.

There are many liming materials available for this purpose, but only four I would recommend: powdered lime, pelleted lime, dolomitic lime, and wood ashes. Others such as burnt and hydrated lime act more quickly, but are hazardous to handle and easy to over-apply. If you choose to use these products, please follow package directions closely.

Pelleted lime is powdered lime that has been mixed with an innocuous water-soluble adhesive for ease of spreading. It acts no more or less quickly than the powdered product, but costs more. Lime can take as long as a year to take full effect, but will remain effective for as long as seven years.

Dolomitic lime contains magnesium in place of some of the calcium. In most soils in the U.S. (excepting clay soils in the Carolinas), its use for up to 1/4 of the liming is beneficial to supply needed magnesium with calcium. It is used at the same rate as regular lime, takes as long to act, and lasts as long.

Wood ashes are a long-neglected soil amendment for pH correction. They contain a wide array of macro-nutrients such as potassium and calcium; but also contain elements such as iron, boron and copper. They act more quickly in correcting soil pH, but do not last as long. Wood ashes are applied at twice the rate of lime for an equal pH correction; but should not be applied at a rate exceeding five pounds per 100 square feet. So, in effect, wood ashes are always used in conjunction with lime, rather than on their own.

The pH scale is a logarithmic value, similar to a decibel. As such, the amount of lime needed to raise the pH from 4 to 5 is greater than the amount of lime needed to raise the pH from 5 to 6. Furthermore, the effectiveness of lime is strongly influenced by the type of soil. So the following table reflects both of these factors. The numbers represent pounds of powdered limestone per 100 square feet. For wood ashes, double that number, but never exceed five pounds per 100 square feet in a given year. Wood ashes can seldom be used exclusively as a pH modifier. Rather, they are best used when mixed with lime. For example, if the table says I need 5.5 lbs of lime, I can use 5 lbs of wood ashes in place of 2.5 lbs of lime, plus 3 lbs of lime.

Pounds of Lime per 100 Square Feet to Correct pH of Acidic Soil				
Measured pH	Sandy	Sand/Loam	Loam	Clay and Clay/Loam
4	5.5	11	16	22
5	3	5.5	11	16
6	1.25	3	3	5.5
7	None	None	None	None

One further note about lime. A lot of sources say you shouldn't apply fertilizer at the same time as lime because the lime will react with the fertilizer and neutralize it. To some extent, this is true. However, lime stays active in the soil for as long as seven years, so the fertilizer will be affected anyway. As long as both are thoroughly incorporated into the soil, don't worry. In addition, these concerns largely pertain to inorganic fertilizers such as ammonium nitrate. When the fertilizers are organic, and composed of such substances as blood meal or alfalfa meal, the adverse effect of the lime is considerably reduced.

Though excessively alkaline (e.g. a pH higher than 6.5) soils are rare in the U.S., they exist in a few places such as the Black Belt prairie region of Alabama, and can be accidentally created through excessive liming.

Correcting an excessively alkaline soil can be done using a variety of substances, including elemental sulfur (known as flowers of sulfur), ammonium sulfate, sulfur coated urea and ammonium nitrate. These substances are seen to be ideal in industrial agriculture, but they are excessively concentrated and can hurt the soil biology, so they aren't recommended for a mini farm aiming at sustainability.

Some authorities also recommend aluminum sulfate, but the levels of aluminum (if the pH ends up changing) can be taken up by the plant and can become toxic to both plants and animals. I recommend either straight flowers of sulfur (if growing organically), or ammonium sulfate (if you don't mind synthetic fertilizers). In practice, the amount of ammonium sulfate required to lower soil pH a given amount is 6.9 times as much as straight sulfur, so you'll likely use sulfur for cost reasons.

Sulfur works by combining with water in the soil to create a weak acid. This acid reacts with alkalies in the soil to form water-soluble salts that are leached from the soil and carried away by rains. Because it creates an acid directly, it is easy to over do sulfur. It should be measured and added carefully, and thoroughly incorporated into the soil. It takes about two months to reach full effectiveness, but results should start to manifest in as little as two weeks.

Sulfur Needed in Pounds per 100 Square Feet to Correct an Alkaline Soil			
Measured pH	Sand	Loam	Clay
8.5	4.6	5.7	6.9
8	2.8	3.4	4.6
7.5	1.1	1.8	2.3
7	0.2	0.4	0.7

Ammonium sulfate works by virtue of the ammonium cation (a positively charged ion) combining with atmospheric oxygen to create two nitrite anions (negatively charged ions), two molecules of water, and four hydrogen cations. These hydrogen cations are the basis for acidity; and they will then acidify the soil.

3

Biochar

Biochar is a benign general soil amendment that enhances the value derived from compost added to your garden. Biochar is a politically correct name for charcoal. Charcoal sounds like (and is) something you'd use to grill burgers, whereas biochar, some say, can save the planet[15]. The difference is that charcoal is burned, releasing

15 Studies on the value of biochar for carbon sequestration are inconsistent. It is, however, good for your garden so I like it!

its carbon into the atmosphere. However, when it is used as a soil amendment, it can sequester carbon for hundreds or even thousands of years. On the scale of a single garden this is unlikely to affect climate change, but it will definitely have a positive effect on soil fertility.

A single gram of powdered charcoal has a surface area of over 500 square meters. Ever since Pierre-Fleurus Touery's dramatic demonstration[16] of the enormous adsorption potential of charcoal to treat poisoning, activated charcoal has been widely used not only for the treatment of ingested poisons but also in gas masks to protect against poison gases and even in water filters. (Activated charcoal has been treated with steam under pressure to increase surface area even further.)

The earliest known use of charcoal as a soil amendment was by the people who inhabited the Amazon prior to the arrival of Columbus.[17] They made their biochar by setting their agricultural waste ablaze in trenches and covering it with soil for it to smolder. Explorers called the dark carbonaceous earth resulting from this practice *terra preta*.

Charcoal is insoluble in water and stable. It has a tremendous unfolded surface area that can provide a home for soil bacteria, help absorb water, and hold nutrients so

---

16 In the mid nineteenth century, Touery demonstrated the value of activated charcoal in treating poisoning by ingesting fifteen grams of activated charcoal simultaneously with a dose of strychnine ten times the lethal dose in the midst of a lecture. At the conclusion of his lecture he walked away unscathed. Strychnine is a deadly neurotoxin.

17 Experts disagree on this. While nobody disagrees on the high fertility of *terra preta*, there is considerable disagreement as to whether biochar was created intentionally as a soil amendment or was an incidental result of creating charcoal as a portable fuel.

they don't wash out of the soil. It can bind with humic substances, thereby improving soil consistency while reducing the rate at which organic matter is depleted from the soil. Overall, it is a real superstar in the garden.[18]

Biochar Application Rate

Pure biochar is benign and can be used to constitute as much as 10 percent of the soil in your garden.[19] The benefits of biochar increase with age, and it lasts hundreds or even thousands of years. Because its value in gardens is derived from its surface area, the addition of any biochar, even as little as one pound per 100 square feet of garden, will yield benefits.

There are no existing guidelines on how much biochar to add to soil based on soil type or crops.[20] In my own tests on beds with low biological activity, it appears that excess amounts of biochar (i.e. exceeding twenty pounds per 100 square feet) can make nutrients less available in the year applied, though the adverse effect diminishes in the second and subsequent years. In my tests on beds with high biological activity, it hasn't been practical for me to add enough biochar to create an adverse

18 Major, Julie et al., "Nutrient Leaching below the Rooting Zone Is Reduced by Biochar, the Hydrology of a Colombian Savanna Oxisol Is Unaffected." (Proc. of North American Biochar Conference 2009, University of Colorado at Boulder. Ithaca: Cornell University Department of Crop and Soil Sciences, 2009. Print.)

19 Elmer, Wade, White, Jason C. and Pignatello, Joseph J., "Impact of Biochar Addition to Soil on the Bioavailability of Chemicals Important in Agriculture." (Rep. New Haven: University of Connecticut, 2009)

20 Major, Julie, *Guidelines on Practical Aspects of Biochar Application to Field Soil in Various Soil Management Systems* (International Biochar Initiative, 2010)

effect because even at forty pounds per 100 square feet, crops grew fine.

I have, however, found a point of diminishing returns. Because biochar doesn't break down and accumulates, you should keep track of the total amount you have added to your garden in your gardening log. Once your annual additions have accumulated to equal ten pounds per 100 square feet, there is no need to add more. There is no measurable difference in yields between beds enriched with ten pounds per 100 square feet and twenty pounds per 100 square feet after five years.

So my summary guideline is to add any amount from one to ten pounds per 100 square feet annually up until a total of ten pounds per 100 square feet have been added. In the future, more research will become available that will result in revision of these guidelines to be sure, because my own tests will necessarily reflect the climate and soils where I tested. Existing research indicates, however, that my recommendations are very conservative and unlikely to pose any risks.

How to Apply Biochar

Biochar is not a fertilizer and it adds absolutely no nutrient content to the soil except whatever may be added incidentally as part of any ash in the biochar. So biochar should be incorporated *in addition to* later recommendations for fertilizer and compost and not in place of them.

Biochar can be incorporated into your soil using the traditional techniques of allowing plant material to smolder in buried trenches, or it can be added as a soil amendment.

The trench method is exactly what the name indicates. Dig a trench about a foot deep and lay the materials you'll be converting to charcoal as flatly in the trench as practical, and light them on fire. (The materials will have to be very dry!) Once the smoke thins out (indicating that the moisture has been driven off and wood is now burning), shovel about an inch of dirt over the materials. This will be enough to reduce the available oxygen so that charcoal is produced rather than having the wood reduced to ash. Once you have reached the charcoal stage, dump water on the materials through the soil to extinguish the fire.

This is a very easy description, but in practice this requires careful observation and a bit of experience to get right, because you can easily end up with either lightly charred wood or completely consumed wood. But once you've done it a couple of times, you'll be an expert. You can do this in a different spot in the garden each time, gradually improving your soil. Over time, soil organisms such as earthworms will distribute and break up the charcoal.

If you are adding biochar as a soil amendment rather than creating it *in situ*, I recommend mixing it with an equal proportion of compost and letting it sit for anywhere from a week to a month before adding to the garden. This is because a lot of its benefit lies in the way it creates a comfortable home for microbes. Distribute your intended amount evenly and then incorporate lightly as with other amendments using a manual three-tined or rotary garden cultivator.

Commercial Sources of Biochar

You can buy hardwood charcoal that is completely natural and has no additives. You'll need to break it up so the pieces are 1/4" or smaller before adding. You can bust it up with a hammer if you'd like. It's a bit of a pain, but if you have kids it can be a pretty good time—just don't forget to wear safety glasses. A faster way to bust up the charcoal briquettes is to line them up on a piece of 2" × 6" lumber that is sitting on a tarp, cover them with a matching piece of lumber, and give it a good solid whack in the center with a sledgehammer. Again, wear safety glasses.

Be absolutely certain that any grilling charcoal you use like this is completely natural and has no additives such as starter fluid or saltpeter (which is used for "self-lighting" charcoal) because you definitely don't want these in your garden soil. Saltpeter is a fertilizer (potassium nitrate) but unless you were planning to use it, its presence can be a problem. Starting fluid is a petroleum product that will leave your garden dead.

There are several manufacturers of biochar, and if you can't get it at a local agricultural store you can have it delivered. Manufactured biochar is bulky, expensive in itself, and expensive to ship. At the time of writing, costs without shipping range from $75 to $240 for enough to cover 100 square feet of garden. That seems excessive to me, though perhaps the price will drop in the future.

Making Your Own Biochar

As described earlier, you can make biochar yourself via the trench method, but you can also use a dedicated pyrolysis setup. "Pyrolysis" is heating something in a low or no oxygen environment so that no combustion takes place. The process of pyrolysis of vegetable matter and wood also produces "biogas" and "bio-oil" that can be collected as alternative energy sources. On a commercial scale, this is very efficient with the heat required for pyrolysis using only 15 percent of the energy produced. On a home scale, it's unlikely these by-products will be collected and hence will escape as atmospheric pollutants. In other words: wood smoke.

Dedicated pyrolysis gear can range from very simple "barrel within barrel" reactors to complex systems for recovery of the expelled gases. Up until petroleum became king, not only was charcoal used extensively in metallurgy to make steel and for heating, the condensed gases were used to make a number of important industrial chemicals such as acetic acid and methyl alcohol. As a result, hundreds of designs for pyrolysis reactors are in the public domain and available over the Internet, and the charcoal they produce can be used as agricultural biochar as well as to grill burgers or make steel.[21]

If you have a wood stove, you can make biochar a little at a time by placing kindling in a small metal container with a single small hole and placing this on top of the logs in the wood stove. After the fire has gone out and the container has cooled, remove the container with some tongs, open it up and you'll have beautiful biochar. The metal containers don't last long unless made of stainless steel. I got mine for $3 at a discount store, but you can purchase suitable containers over the Internet by searching for stainless steel retorts. (In chemistry or chemical manufacturing, a retort is a vessel heated to facilitate a chemical reaction or for distillation.)

---

21 Hugh McLaughlin and Doug Clayton have put the Jolly Roger series of biochar-making devices into the public domain. If you want biochar on a large scale, their devices are exhaustively documented with videos, pictures and instructions available via any Internet search engine.

Making Biochar in a Wood Stove

Materials

- Wood stove
- Wood
- Stainless steel container with one small hole or suitable retort
- Kindling

Procedure

1. Set your paper, cardboard, kindling and logs in your wood stove, but don't light it.
2. Pack your retort with kindling.
3. Set your covered retort in the wood stove on top of your logs.
4. Run the wood stove. Don't add any more wood and let the fire go out on its own.
5. When the stove and retort are cool, remove the retort, open it, and examine your biochar.

⊗ Retort packed with kindling.

⊗ Retort upright in the stove.

⊗ Temperatures exceeding 700°F are optimal.

⊗ This biochar has a bit of ash and some sparks.

6. If any biochar is smoldering, douse with water and drain.

7. Break up the biochar into small pieces. I put the biochar in a plastic bag and break it up using a rolling pin.

⊗ Biochar after dousing.

⊗ Breaking up the biochar with a rolling pin.

4

Compost Science and the Nutrient Cycle

Composting is easy, but no matter how easy something is, a bit of background information is helpful and can enhance efforts to be more self-sufficient.

Perhaps one of the most important physical laws for the gardener is the law of Conservation of Matter. In the nuclear age, because matter can become energy and vice versa,[22] it is called

---

22 $e = mc^2$ is perhaps the most famous equation in existence. What this equation describes is the energy content (e in ergs) of a given mass (m in grams) of matter. Matter can become energy and energy can become matter.

the law of Conservation of Matter and Energy. But unless you have a nuclear reactor out back, transformations of matter and energy won't need to be considered as their contribution is so small it can't be practically measured.

Everything we can see, feel, taste, or smell is made of matter. That matter can be composed of numerous compounds. For example, black gunpowder is made from charcoal, sulfur and potassium nitrate (saltpeter), all intimately mixed in proper proportions so that it appears to be a homogeneous substance, even though it is a mixture.

Potassium nitrate has the chemical formula KNO_3. This means it is composed of three fundamental elements: potassium (K), nitrogen(N) and oxygen(O). The sulfur in gunpowder is the element sulfur (S) and the charcoal is primarily a source of the element carbon (C).

Natural philosophers discovered that in a closed system, the total amount of any given element in that system never changes, no matter how the material is transformed. When black gunpowder is used in a gun, for example, though it may cease to exist as gunpowder, all of its constituent elements are re-combined into new compounds. The chemical formula for this deflagration is:

$$10KNO_3 + 3S + 8C \rightarrow 2K_2CO_3 + 3K_2SO_4 + 6CO_2 + 5N_2$$

The total number of atoms of each element in the black gunpowder stays the same, even when the powder has exploded. This identical principle applies to the compounds in your garden, though hopefully with a lot less noise or danger.

Plants obtain elements from their environment such as carbon dioxide from the air, and other elements from water and soil. Through photosynthesis and mechanisms of life, those elements are transformed into millions of compounds used by plants in their life processes. The carbon, hydrogen and oxygen used to create vitamin C initially come from water absorbed by the roots and carbon dioxide absorbed from the atmosphere.

Plants also obtain numerous other elements from the soil, including calcium, magnesium, boron, molybdenum, sulfur and more. When you eat some portion of the plant, some of those elements are retained in your body, and others are eliminated in exhaled air, feces, sweat or urine. When these elements are retained in your body or eliminated and not recaptured, they are lost to your soil and will need an external source of replenishment.

But those portions of a plant that aren't consumed stay in the ground. Depending upon the plant, that may constitute the majority of the plant's matter, such as with tomatoes. Or, as with spinach, it may be very little. But if you put what remains of the plant into your compost pile, the elements contained in those remains will become incorporated into your compost so when you add the finished compost back into your beds, the elements are returned to the soil. This will conserve a surprising quantity of elements and will drastically reduce the amount of amendments you will need to add to your soil, thereby reducing your costs and also increasing the micro-nutrient content of your food, making it more healthful.

But composting is imperfect. There is no such thing as a perfectly sustainable system. Indeed, through entropy, eventually the Sun will grow cold and the Earth will move through space devoid of life. Thankfully, that is billions of years in the future, but the point is that there is no such thing as perfect sustainability, which means that in practice no matter how diligently you compost, certain nutrients will need to be added from time to time.

You can add those nutrients to your garden by incorporating them directly into your soil. Or, you can put additional material into your compost that didn't come from your garden, or a combination of the two.

As my garden is in my yard, and my yard requires mowing—I use a bag on the lawnmower to catch the cut grass and throw that on my compost pile. (I use the term "grass" generically because my yard contains a lot of weeds. I like it that way because of their diverse nutrient uptake.) There are also a lot of trees around my yard that shed leaves. Large trees will sink roots that gather ample micro-nutrients, many of which are present in the leaves. I rake those up and put them in my compost pile. Then I add my organic kitchen refuse such as egg shells, orange peels and so forth.

Because I don't live too far from the beach, at times I have gathered seaweed in five gallon buckets and dragged those home to put on the compost pile. Not surprisingly, my chicken manure goes in the compost pile, along with any chicken entrails from processing chickens for meat. When I clean the old hay out of the chicken coop, that goes on the compost pile too.

Consequently, my compost pile looks big compared to the size of my garden. It is massively supplemented with leaves, grass clippings, table scraps and more.

Because of all this supplementation, my compost contains a wide array of nutrients in sufficient amounts. This helps to reduce the nutrients that would need to be added to the beds dramatically.

This, then, is the secret of compost and the nutrient cycle. When I add compost to the beds in the spring or fall, I wait for it to be well incorporated for a couple of weeks before testing my soil for macro-nutrients: nitrogen, phosphorus and potassium.

When I add nutrients, I add them in a form that also includes trace elements. For example, if my beds need potassium, I will add some greensand, kelp meal and wood ashes. Wood ashes contain calcium, potassium, magnesium, sulfur, phosphorus, manganese, zinc, iron, boron and more.[23] Greensand contains more than thirty trace elements in addition to silicon, iron, potassium and magnesium. Though kelp meal doesn't have tons of potassium, using it as a source for at least part of your potassium will be beneficial as 33 percent of its weight in aggregate is composed of trace elements including iodine, beryllium, silver and chromium among others.

The primary source of phosphorus in a mini farm is compost. But if phosphorus is needed, in order to also incorporate micro-nutrients, it could be added in the form of either phosphate rock or bone meal. Bone meal contains nitrogen, along with calcium, phosphorus, iodine, boron, copper, zinc, iron and other elements. Phosphate rock contains phosphorus, calcium, selenium, molybdenum, cobalt, antimony, arsenic, tin and other trace elements.

Of particular concern with phosphate rock is that it contains naturally occurring radioactive elements including polonium 210.[24] I am not personally concerned about other poisonous

23 Misra, M. K., Ragland, K. W. and Baker, A. J., "Wood Ash Composition as a Function of Furnace Temperature", *Biomass and Bioenery* 4;2 (1993): 103–16

24 Bech, J. et al., "Selenium and other trace elements in phosphate rock of Nayovar-Sechura (Peru)", *Journal of Geochemical Exploration*, 107 (November 2010): 136–45

elements in phosphate rock such as arsenic, because even though in excess they are quite deadly and arsenic particularly is carcinogenic, small amounts (as little as 0.01 mg/day) are needed by the body. I am, however, concerned about the radioactive elements, including polonium 210. Polonium 210 from phosphate rock is known to concentrate in tobacco, contributing to its danger, and can enter humans via food sources.[25] Because of this concern, I have never added phosphate rock to my beds. But phosphate rock is considerably less expensive than bone meal, so if you decide to use it, I would recommend using it no more often than once every five years. Cave bat guano and fossilized sea bird guano, if you can find them at a reasonable price, are also good sources of phosphorus that are high in trace elements.

After your first couple of years, conscientious composting will, in most cases, give you plenty of phosphorus and potassium in your beds or garden. The major macro-nutrient you'll need to replenish is nitrogen. In general, I recommend using two or more sources of nitrogen so you get something fast acting and also something that breaks down more slowly to deliver nitrogen over time. I also recommend avoiding fresh animal manures (even though they contain nitrogen) because they can transmit diseases and weed seeds.

Slow sources of nitrogen include: composted poultry manure or compost that contains manure, alfalfa meal, soybean meal, cottonseed meal, feather meal and green manures. "Green manure" is a fancy way of saying "cover crops". Cover crops that fix nitrogen include all legumes, such as vetch, clover, alfalfa,

---

25 Hill, C. R., "Polonium-210 Content of Human Tissues in Relation to Dietary Habit", *Science* 152 (3726): 1261–2

peas and beans. If they are cut before they set seed, the roots remaining in the ground will slowly release nitrogen to subsequently planted crops, and the above-ground portion can be added to the compost pile.[26] Fast acting nitrogen sources include dried blood, fish emulsion and fish meal. These tend to be expensive, but they are very concentrated.

Taken in aggregate, these natural sources of nitrogen, phosphorus and potassium also include many trace elements. When natural sources of fertility such as these are added to your beds, the beds will also concentrate the trace elements. These trace elements along with macro-nutrients are conserved by composting the crop debris each season, and adding the resulting compost back to the beds.

Compost is the most cost-effective way to conserve and add nutrients in the long run, because compost is a complex living substance that holds onto nutrients in a biological matrix, releasing those nutrients to plants on an as-needed basis. Because the nutrients are held by living organisms, they aren't washed out of the soil as water-soluble fertilizers would be.

So the nutrient cycle in your soil can be summarized as follows:

1. You start with the existing soil in your garden, supplement with compost (either homemade or purchased), wait a couple of weeks (or until spring if compost was added in the fall), and test your soil for NPK using a testing kit.

---

26 For more information on cover cropping, please see my book *Mini Farming: Self Sufficiency on ¼ Acre.*

2. You supplement your soil's NPK as needed with organic amendments based on soil test results.
3. You grow your crops. Some fertility is lost due to crops consumed or sold. The crop refuse is added to your compost pile, along with lawn clippings, leaves, manure from animals and other organic materials.
4. Your material is composted. After being composted, it is added back to your beds.
5. Start again at step one.

Biology and Chemistry of Compost

The world is covered with microorganisms—bacteria, protozoans, viruses, fungi, and more. In fact, the surface and intestinal tract of the human body contain ten times as many cells from microorganisms as human cells. These microorganisms are, for the most part, beneficial and assist us in digesting foods such as the inulin in Jerusalem artichokes, also helping to make vitamins such as B12. Science is just beginning to understand the role and importance gut microbes play in human health, but there is now evidence that they may even play a role in behavior.[27,28]

Microbes in the soil are just as important. Under natural conditions, microbes incorporate elements such as phosphorus and nitrogen in their protoplasm, and release these to the roots

---

27 Bailey, M. T. et al., "Exposure to a social stressor alters the structure of the intestinal microbiota: implications for stressor-induced immunomodulation", Brain, Behavior, and Immunity, 25;3 (March 2011): 397–407
28 Marshall, J., "Are Gut Bacteria In Charge? Microbes in our bellies may be telling us to eat more, determining how much we move, and making us anxious", Discovery News, Oct 26 2011

of plants in exchange for the plants providing glucose. Beneficial soil microbes also create compounds that fight off diseases that would otherwise harm the plants that feed them. One reason cover crops are so important in natural gardening is that they keep the microbes in the soil fed and healthy between crops.

Just as microbes exist on our skin, they exist on the surfaces of plants. Each person harbors slightly different bacteria on their skin or within the digestive tract depending upon various dietary, immune, environmental and genetic factors – and the same applies to plants. During life, these microbes are generally benign and are often beneficial in that they discourage less benign species from establishing a foothold. This is why some people are prone to yeast infections after being treated with antibiotics: the antibiotics kill beneficial microbes that were keeping pathogenic species in check. A healthy plant is surrounded with microbes all the way from roots to flowers.

An interesting phenomenon is that the natural microbes that help so much during life also happen to be the ideally matched microbes for decomposing the wastes of a given animal or the remains of a plant or animal that has died. These microbes consist of hundreds of species, some of which require oxygen to work and some of which don't. Likewise, some of the microbes work best at low temperatures of 0°F through 55°F (psychrophilic), whereas others work best at temperatures between 50°F and 113°F (mesophilic) or 104°F to 160°F (thermophilic). So any waste product or dead plant or animal will ultimately decompose, albeit at different rates and with different results, at any temperature between 0°F and 170°F, whether oxygen is present or not. This is one of the reasons why frozen food will only stay palatable for a certain length of time. Nature is very eager to have its elements back!

When you build a compost pile, you are combining materials along with the microbes required to decompose them. Hence, all by themselves and with no intervention whatsoever, they will ultimately turn into compost. However, a haphazard approach may suit nature's needs but won't necessarily meet your needs in the garden because it could fail to get rid of pathogenic microbes and weed seeds, or it could take years to fully break down. The whole point of taking a conscious hand in composting is to work with nature in such a way as to meet your needs in the garden. To do this, a bit of basic knowledge is helpful.[29]

There are two basic ways to make compost: aerobically (requiring oxygen) and anaerobically (not requiring oxygen). Aerobic composting is the most popular in gardening because it offers the option of thermophilic approaches that will raise the temperature of the pile high enough to kill off weed seeds and pathogens, and it also produces mature compost more quickly and without disagreeable smells. Aerobic compost consumes oxygen and water, and gives off carbon dioxide.

Anaerobic composting is nearly always at mesophilic temperatures. Septic tanks are a great example of anaerobic composting, and the smell of a septic tank is remarkably similar to that of anaerobic compost being made because both produce methane, ammonia and various gases containing sulfur along with compounds such as indole and skatole. It takes longer to work and doesn't kill pathogens as quickly. A haphazardly

---

29 Bacon, Francis, "Human knowledge and human power meet in one; for where the cause is not known the effect cannot be produced. Nature to be commanded must be obeyed; and that which in contemplation is as the cause is in operation as the rule." *Novum Organum*, (1620), Aphorism 3

⊗ As compost breaks down, it shrinks considerably. This pile will be turned soon.

managed compost pile that is intended to be aerobic will some-times go anaerobic, and you can tell by the smell. Turning the compost thoroughly will remedy that.

Microbes, just like plants, need a certain mix of nutrients to properly perform. Like other organisms, their RNA and DNA are organic molecules containing carbon. RNA and DNA are com-posed of amino acids, and amino acids also contain nitrogen and carbon. Naturally, for all their various proteins, cellular struc-tures and enzymes, they require other elements as well, but the primary elements that need to be managed in composting are carbon and nitrogen. The ratio of carbon to nitrogen in the pile needs to be managed differently for aerobic and anaerobic com-posting, with the latter requiring more nitrogen than the former. In addition, within aerobic piles, the carbon to nitrogen ratio affects the temperature of the pile by mediating the presence of materials needed for thermophilic bacteria to reproduce.

All composting creates heat, but the amount of heat cre-ated depends upon the type of composting. In this respect, you can think in terms of chemical reactions rather than microbes. Aerobic composting oxidizes carbon to carbon dioxide. This is like a flame, except it occurs at a slower rate. The starches in plants are composed of chains of glucose. A single gram of glucose that is oxidized to carbon dioxide generates enough heat to raise the temperature of 500 kilograms of compost by 34°F.

In contrast, the carbon in anaerobic composting is converted to methane, CH_4. Instead of releasing energy as heat, the process instead stores that energy in the chemical bonds between carbon and hydrogen. Anaerobic composting processes are used to generate methane for heating and energy. So in anaerobic composting, a single gram of glucose only generates enough heat to raise the temperature of thirty kilograms of compost by 34°F.

Different materials within compost are broken down at different rates. Though bacteria will ultimately degrade cellulose, during high temperature phases when bacteria are most active they predominantly break down proteins and simple carbohydrates, while cellulose and lignin[30] seem barely affected. Greater breakdown of these occurs after the thermophilic phase has ended and actinomycetes and fungi predominate. Actinomycetes are what give compost that fresh and earthy smell.

As with most chemical and biological processes, the smaller the starting particles, the faster they will break down. This is because more surface area is exposed per unit of mass. Sawdust breaks down more quickly than a log, for example. Though equipment such as a chipper or shredder is certainly not necessary, if you happen to have one and use it, the compost will be ready more quickly.

---

30 Lignin is a heterogenous polymer that exists in cross-links with cellulose molecules and assists plants with water transport. Lignin is largely responsible for the structural strength and durability of wood.

>> Because of its micro-nutrient content, seaweed gathered from the beach is a valuable addition to compost.

Pathogen Destruction

Pathogen destruction is a major concern with compost, especially compost created on a large scale (such as a municipality) where it is impossible to assess whether the starting ingredients have various forms of contamination. But even in a home garden, the parasite-infested family cat may use a garden bed as a litter box, your squash may get powdery mildew or a bird with avian flu may leave droppings on material you compost. It is even more of a concern if any of the material had a human origin, such as human feces, because many pathogens spread that way, and they wouldn't have to jump species to pose a risk. Likewise, chickens are often carriers for salmonella and other pathogens, and their manure could be infective.

Pathogen destruction in composting is affected by four things: time, temperature, hostile environment and lack of a suitable host.

No known human pathogen (or spoor for such a pathogen) can survive temperatures exceeding 140°F for more than a few minutes. Aerobic composting that is thermophilic can reach such temperatures if properly managed, and thus creates compost that is free of pathogens sooner than other methods.

Most pathogens are adapted to a particular biological niche and don't fare very well outside of that niche. For example, Neisseria meningitidis will survive for a day and a half at most outside the body, and the survival of Mycoplasma pneumoniae outside the body won't exceed five days.[31] A compost pile, no matter how it is managed, won't be a breeding ground for such pathogens.

However, even though the environment of a compost pile may not be the preferred host for a pathogen, that doesn't mean it can't persist for a long time if the pile is not thermophilic. Anthrax, botulism and tetanus form spoors so they can survive in unfriendly environments until a suitable host is encountered. In addition, many pathogenic bacteria that do not form spoors can survive for a long time. For example, Corynebacterium diphteriae can persist in room temperature soil for as long as 208 days.[32] (Incidentally, the longer a pathogen can survive in the environment, the more quickly it can be lethal.)

This leads us to the importance of time as a factor in creating pathogen-free compost. Once compost is finished, it should be held for a certain period of time before use in order to assure the death of pathogens. How long it needs to be held depends on the method used. Thermophilic aerobic compost

---

31 Walther B. A. and Ewald P. W., "Pathogen survival in the external environment and the evolution of virulence", *Biol. Rev.*, 79 (2004): 849–69

32 Laurell, G. et al., "Airborne infections. 2. A report on the methods.", *Acta Medica Scandinavica* 134 (1949): 189–204

should be aged at least three months after it is ready. Mesophilic aerobic compost should be held for an additional six months. Anaerobic compost should be held for a year. These holding times provide a safety factor for the disappearance of pathogens either due to temperature or the inhospitable environment.

During the time of composting and holding, inter-species microbial warfare creates an inhospitable environment. Antibiotics that are commonly used to treat pathogenic infections in humans and animals have their origin in microbes. Penicillin is produced by a mold, Penicillium, in order to keep competing bacteria and mold from invading its food supply. Erythromycin is derived from Streptomyces erthreus, bacitracin is made by

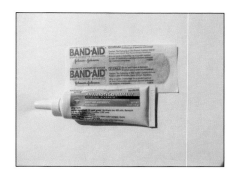

❂ Many common antibiotics are derived from microbes found in compost and soil.

Bacillus subtilis, polymyxin comes from Bacillus polymyxa and gentamicin is derived from Micromonospora purpurea.

Only a small fraction of the antibiotics made by molds and bacteria have been applied to uses in humans or animals. In some cases, they won't make it through stomach acids intact or have adverse side-effects that preclude their use. In other cases, they have never been isolated and explored. Either way, the microbial world generates thousands of different antibiotics within a compost pile, each one with its own spectrum and mechanism of action. Thus, given time, the pathogens are destroyed.

It's interesting that, at the time antibiotics were discovered, most authorities believed that development of resistance would take hundreds of years. This turned out to be far from correct, with antibiotic resistant infections now constituting the fourth leading cause of death in the country.[33] There are a couple of reasons for this. Even though we may not understand how it thinks or behaves, every living organism on this planet has undergone 3.5 billion years of trial-by-fire, and in its own way is a highly intelligent evolutionary pinnacle. Bacteria have dealt with antibiotics for all of evolution, and they still exist. Ergo, they have well-developed mechanisms for adapting to deal with them. The second is that human application of antibiotics is usually just a single antibiotic with a single mode of action, allowing bacteria to adapt via only one modification.[34]

You don't have to worry about this problem in your compost pile. The number of antibiotics present is mindboggling, and anything susceptible to being killed through those antibiotics has been killed by so many different mechanisms that the simultaneous development of resistance to all of them at once is not going to happen. In fact, studies have shown that composting cattle manure containing antibiotics and antibiotic resistant bacteria eliminates the antibiotics and kills the bacteria.

In addition, many antibiotics in nature work via mechanisms that would make them deadly to an animal host. These

---

33 Buhrer, S.H., *Herbal Antibiotics* (2011)
34 Insecticide resistance is common in pests. In my book *Mini Farming: Self Sufficiency on ¼ Acre*, I advocate using organic insecticides that work via different mechanisms together in order to avoid the development of resistance. Composting does the same thing on a microbial scale.

can't be used to treat infections, but a compost pile will generate them as part of microbial warfare.

However, those antibiotics do not kill *all* bacteria. If they did, the bacteria responsible for composting wouldn't survive.

Pathogens and Composted Manure

There is a very big exception to pathogen destruction: E. coli. Most variations of E. coli are perfectly harmless, and in fact we all carry E. coli in our digestive tracts where it produces vitamin K2 and prevents infections from other bacteria. But some variations of E. coli make devastating toxins that can kill. E. coli is generally believed to have a short survival time and an inability to reproduce outside of the bodies of warm-blooded animals, and it is therefore used as a marker for testing water supplies for fecal contamination. Unfortunately, this belief is not based on fact.

It is interesting how little cross over there is in knowledge between different branches of science. The standards for testing water are based on the idea that E. coli in water or soil cannot be native, and must therefore result from relatively recent introduction of feces. The reality is that E. coli is an amazingly adaptable organism. It can carry on its metabolism via both aerobic and anaerobic pathways, can survive across a wide temperature range and can adapt to an extremely wide array of food sources. As a result, some variants of E. coli can easily become naturalized in soil, water and silt.[35]

---

35 Ishii, S. and Sadowsky, M. "Escherichia coli in the Environment: Implications for Water Quality and Human Health, *Microbes and Environments* 23;2 (2008): 101–8

Though anaerobic composting will, in fact, destroy most pathogens including salmonella given time, septic tanks (the most common form of anaerobic composting) are the primary source of E. coli contamination of well water. There are some intriguing studies that seem to show that the variants of E. coli that inhabit septic tanks are genetically distinct from the E. coli that inhabits the intestines of those who use the tanks,[36] but the high levels of E. coli in anaerobically composted septic effluent nevertheless indicate that fecal matter that is composted anaerobically shouldn't be applied to actively growing crops—especially those eaten raw. Certainly, anaerobically produced compost that contains feces can be rendered sterile through the subsequent thorough application of sufficient heat, but this would not be efficient on anything less than an industrial scale.

In general, it would be expected that the antibiotics produced in composting would ultimately get rid of the E. coli. But even in aerobic compost at mesophilic temperatures (e.g. under 90°F), numerous studies have shown that E. coli can survive for at least several weeks. Given the capacity of E. coli to become naturalized, I do not believe you should trust mesophilic aerobic composting to sufficiently reduce E. coli levels for safety.

Therefore, I believe that anaerobically composted animal manures or mesophilic aerobically composted animal manures should be treated *just like fresh manure* in terms of being applied to soil. That is, it should be applied to soil (and never to an actively growing crop) not less than 120 days

---

36 Gordon D. M., Bauer, S. and Johnson, J. R., "The genetic structure of Escherichia coli populations in primary and secondary habitats", *Microbiology*, 148;5 (May 2002): 1513–22

prior to the harvest of the crop. This is the standard for application of fresh manure in the regulations governing organic agriculture, and that standard has been rigorously tested for safety. Given that much time in the outdoors, the UV-C radiation from the sun will kill the E. coli on the soil surface and soil microbes will wipe out the E. coli so that crops eaten raw will be safe.

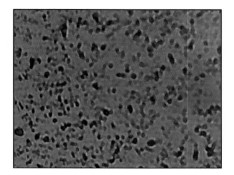

⊗ E. coli and other bacteria from a fecal sample.[37]

The national organic program guidelines require that compost containing animal manures reach temperatures of between 131°F and 170°F for at least three days during the composting process. At a temperature of 131°F, all known human pathogens are destroyed within a day and, at a temperature of 140°F, all known human pathogens are destroyed within an hour. The best recommended practice for composting animal manure is to use aerobic thermophilic composting in which temperatures exceeding 140°F are maintained for at least three days over the course of composting, and in which the pile is turned at least a couple of times so that unheated materials from the outer layers of the pile are brought to the inside of the pile and heated. Using this method, E. coli will not survive more than a week so the resultant compost can be safely used on actively growing crops.

---

37 Three-gram fecal sample fermented one day in 30 ml distilled water. Heat fixation followed by methylene blue stain for two minutes. Magnified x400.

Prions

There is one type of pathogen that is not destroyed even by the best thermophilic composting: the prion. A prion is a rogue protein fragment whose three-dimensional structure will cause nearby proteins to adopt the same structure, thereby replicating itself and destroying the function of the proteins.

Prion diseases can occur spontaneously or due to hereditary factors, but the largest concern is that they can be transmitted from animal to human hosts through the consumption of the animal's brains. Deer, cattle and squirrels have all been implicated. The diseases caused by prions are rare in humans but invariably fatal after a long incubation period after which they destroy brain tissue.

Prions can only be rendered non-infective through complete denaturing involving bleach, strong acids, strong bases and complete incineration. Therefore, you shouldn't try to compost any material with a reasonable likelihood of containing prions. In practice, don't compost the heads or brains of any mammals likely infected with a prion illness such as CWD (chronic wasting disease) or mad cow disease in your pile. If you have to dispose of such things, commercial incineration is the best option.

Moisture Content

The amount of water in compost is important for several reasons. At a macroscopic scale, the amount of water present will determine whether a composting process will be aerobic or anaerobic, because water beyond a certain level will effectively exclude air from the spaces between particles in the compost. Excluding air would make the compost anaerobic.

At a microscopic level, water is a fundamental prerequisite of life and therefore adequate levels need to be maintained for the health of microbes in the pile. Furthermore, water is the source of the hydrogen used in the synthesis of biological compounds such as DNA.

You can "eyeball" water levels in your compost easily enough. For anaerobic compost, you want it wet enough that if you grab a handful and squeeze, water will leak out. For aerobic compost, you want it wet enough to feel damp and for particles to clump together, but not so wet that water leaks out when squeezed. If your compost is too wet, turn it and add a bit of drier material. If it is too dry, turn it and add water (if it is aerobic compost) or just soak it down good with a hose and cover it (if it is anaerobic compost.)

There is no magical percentage of moisture that works in all cases, because each material can absorb a different amount of moisture while still having air pockets and spaces for air contact. For aerobic composting, a range of 45 percent to 60 percent water by weight is considered ideal, whereas for anaerobic composting 70 percent is the usual target level. Again, these aren't cast in stone and will vary based on the materials in the compost.

Moisture content of compost can also be predicted by measuring the moisture content of the materials you plan to include in the compost.

Measuring Material Moisture Content

Materials Needed

- Scale, accurate to within 0.1 gram
- 250 ml beaker OR small plastic cup
- The material to be tested

Procedure

Weigh the empty beaker or cup and record the mass. Fill the beaker with the material and weigh it, recording the mass. Now, place the beaker and sample in an oven set at 220°F– 230°F for twenty-four hours. Weigh it again and record the mass. You can now calculate the percentage moisture in the material with the following formula:

C = mass of empty container
W = mass of container and raw material
D = mass of container with dried material

$$\text{Moisture percentage} = (((W-C)-(D-C))/(W-C)) \times 100$$

Once you know the moisture percentage of the materials, you can calculate the aggregate moisture content of your compost when those materials are added together as follows:

M1 = Moisture percentage of first material
W1 = Weight of first material
M2 = Moisture percentage of second material
W2 = Weight of second material

$$\text{Compost Moisture \%} = ((M1 \times W1) + (M2 \times W2) + \ldots)/(W1 + W2 + \ldots)$$

Obviously, these equations are only useful if you have large quantities of substances (such as leaves in the fall or grass clippings) that you plan to use to make a compost pile. With a bit of algebra, and if you know your target moisture level, you can re-arrange the equation to tell you how much leaf matter to mix into your grass clippings. If you can't hit your desired moisture level, you will still have a good indication of how much water will need to be added, figuring water at a weight of eight pounds per gallon.

Carbon/Nitrogen Ratio

In chemistry, the term "organic" refers to compounds that contain carbon. In agriculture, the term "organic" refers to natural methodologies. But in both cases, the word has its origin in the chemistry of living things. Living things require both carbon and nitrogen. The carbon makes up the backbone of the various compounds necessary for life, and the nitrogen is necessary for the amine group that defines an amino acid. Amino acids form the building blocks of life itself in the forms of RNA and DNA along with the proteins used for cellular processes and more.

Living things require much more carbon than nitrogen. The amino acid tryptophan, for example, contains eleven carbon atoms, and only two nitrogen atoms. Other elements besides carbon and nitrogen are also required to make amino

⊗ Dried leaves are a valuable carbon source for compost.

acids, such as oxygen, sulfur, phosphorus and hydrogen. Living things generally derive their sustenance from other living things (or the refuse of other living things). This means that instead of carbon and nitrogen being used directly, they

 Grass clippings are a good source of nitrogen in your compost pile.

are taken from other more complex substances such as sugars and proteins. As a result, when microbes in compost have access to carbon and nitrogen in the correct ratios, they also automatically have access to other elements that are needed. As a result, compost can be optimized by adjusting carbon/nitrogen ratio broadly, without worrying about the details of elements such as sulfur.

The reason why carbon/nitrogen ratio is important is because if either is deficient, it will place a limit on microbial reproduction. Having the ratio right for the type of composting technique being used will result in finished compost more quickly, and will also allow thermophilic compost to attain optimum temperatures for pathogen destruction.

At most, the microbes in a compost pile will convert 35 percent of the carbon in the pile into humus, with the remaining 65 percent being converted by microbial metabolism into carbon dioxide that is released into the atmosphere.

Don't be concerned about greenhouse gases because by composting you are simply changing the *location* in which composting takes place. By managing for optimal C/N ratio, you are in fact maximizing the amount of carbon that is sequestered into humus and minimizing the amount going into the atmosphere. So in terms of greenhouse gas emissions, composting can improve somewhat on nature. It's important to see the big picture. When you grow your own food, you are also cutting down on the emissions of trucks, farm machinery and a host of other sources; the items you compost would have generated carbon dioxide while decomposing anyway.

The optimal C/N ratio for aerobic compost is 25–30:1. This will provide for the most rapid thermophilic decomposition for pathogen destruction while preserving as much nitrogen as possible. Aerobic composts at mesophilic temperatures can have ratios as high as 50:1. Such piles will take a very long time (as long as two years) to be ready for use, whereas a thermophilic aerobic pile can produce cured compost in as little as three months. An excess of nitrogen, that is C/N ratios lower than 25:1, is ideal for fast anaerobic composting. In fact, if your C/N ratio is too low, you'll have a hard time turning a pile enough to keep it aerobic during the initial stages.

Theoretically, the carbon/nitrogen ratio can be directly managed by controlling what goes into the compost pile. However, most of us put what we have into the pile and then work with the results. What I recommend is two outdoor compost piles: one that is thermophilic and another that could be either mesophilic or anaerobic. By using two piles with two different carbon/nitrogen ratio requirements, you can allocate source materials in a fashion that is optimum for each. Each source material has a different C/N ratio, and the table on the following page will give you approximate information to help with your allocation.

"Green" Materials				"Brown" Materials			
Substance	C/N Ratio	Density (lbs per ft³)	Moisture %	Substance	C/N Ratio	Density (lbs per ft³)	Moisture %
Grass clippings	17	-	82	Hay	90	8	12
Chicken manure	7	55	69	Leaves	70	7	38
Food scraps	17	50+	69	Sawdust	325	15	39
Vegetable scraps	12	58	87	Wood chips	400	8	20
Cow manure	20	55	81	Peat moss	58	7	-
Fruit waste	32	50+	80	Corn stalks	60	1	13
Fresh weeds	20	-	65	Shredded news-paper	175	5	8
Seaweed	19	-	-	Shrub trimmings	53	15	16
Garden soil	10	34	-				

If you are building a pile from scratch by adding a lot of material all at once (such as mowing the lawn and raking the leaves), you can get within the ballpark of the right C/N ratio by adding greens and browns in 2:1 proportions by weight. That is, for every 100 pounds of a "green," add another 50 pounds of a "brown." The math works out pretty well without regard to the exact items. Using grass clippings and leaves, the resulting C/N ratio is 35. If you use chicken manure and hay, the resulting C/N ratio is also 35. Still, it is good to take a look at the table and adjust a bit, because if you are adding wood chips with a C/N ratio of 400, you will need to add 16 pounds of grass clippings for every pound of wood chips.

❧ If you have chickens or other livestock, their manure is a valuable addition to your compost.

If you add to your piles a little at a time like most people, the best avenue is to add greens and browns in a 1:1 ratio by weight. The reason is because, initially, the pile doesn't have enough mass to retain heat, so trying to get the ratio right to make it go thermophilic will actually result in slimy anaerobic compost. There's nothing wrong with slimy anaerobic compost, of course. But if you are trying to make aerobic compost and you add material a little at a time, add greens and browns in an approximate 1:1 ratio, so you'll end up with mesophilic aerobic compost. Once you stop adding to the pile, you can always turn it thermophilic by adding a nitrogen source in layers as you turn it. (See "green" materials in the table for nitrogen sources.)

When composting indoors, you want your ratio right at the very beginning to keep down smells. You can figure out how much of a given "green" is needed to counterbalance a pound of a brown and have a particular C/N ratio with the following equation:

P = Pounds of the green to be added per pound of the brown

B = C/N ratio of the brown

G = C/N ratio of the green

R = Desired C/N ratio

$$P = (B - R)/(R - G)$$

For example, how many pounds of cow manure would I need to add to a pound of sawdust if I want a final C/N ratio of 30? Looking at the table, B = 325 and G = 20. We already know that R = 30, so . . .

$$P = (325 - 30)/(30 - 20) = 29.5$$

How many pounds of chicken manure would I need to mix with a pound of hay to give me a C/N ratio of 25?

$$P = (90 - 25)/(25 - 7) = 3.6$$

Humic Substances

I have described that bacteria either hold onto nutrients in their protoplasm and release them to plants as needed, or convert the nutrients from inaccessible organic to organic forms.

This is true, but there is more. The process of composting creates a product rich in humic and fulvic acids. These are created by bacteria as they decompose materials such as lignin. The terms used in describing these compounds—humic acids, fulvic acids, humates and humic chelates—are inexact. Rather than describing precise compounds, they describe a class of compounds with common average characteristics.

As a class, humic and fulvic acids are complex and comprise an array of compounds that include phenolic rings and carboxylate groups acting as dibasic or tribasic acids. These can form complexes or chelates with the ions of nutrients such as magnesium, calcium and iron. Because of the unique distribution of charges on these structures, they can form super-molecules of large size similar to polymers of plastic that lend both structure and water-holding capacity to soil.

Thus, along with bacteria and fungi, humic substances play an important role in regulating the availability of important metallic and non-metallic elements such as iron and calcium for plants. Humic substances will keep soils from becoming hard or forming a crust that discourages seedling emergence, and they help form channels that allow water to penetrate more deeply and mitigate erosion while allowing oxygen to reach roots for better root growth. When added to the soil, these humic substances help to sustain healthy bacteria (such as nitrogen fixation bacteria), provide growth enhancers, discourage the growth of harmful organisms and encourage the growth of helpful organisms.

Interestingly, though the precise composition of the humic and fulvic acid complexes produced through composting will vary with starting ingredients and composting technique, the aggregate characteristics of the end product are quite similar. Finished compost contains a mixture of these humic substances with various bacteria, small particles of matter, antibiotics and other compounds.

5

Anaerobic Composting

I have never seen a gardening book discuss anaerobic composting in any context other than how to avoid it. This is a bit odd, considering that far more people own anaerobic composters than any other kind. The most common form of anaerobic composting is the septic tank ubiquitously installed in suburban and rural areas. The second most common form in the home is a compost pile that is intended to be aerobic but has been mismanaged. Nature loves anaerobic composting and the marsh gas in marshes results from the anaerobic composting that takes place at the bottom of swamps and bogs.

The term "anaerobic" means "without air" or, most commonly, "without oxygen." Anaerobic composting has some advantages in that it is the easiest way to compost and preserves the greatest physical volume of compost compared to other methods while requiring the least work and intervention. It also has some disadvantages in that it takes longer to mature, does not dispose of pathogens through heat and, most importantly, smells nauseatingly horrendous. Many folk intending to make aerobic compost do some anaerobic composting accidentally when they fail to turn their piles or their piles become saturated with water due to torrential rains. If you go out to turn your compost pile and find it to be slimy with a disgusting smell—congratulations, you've been making anaerobic compost unintentionally! Turning and aerating your pile will help bring it back to an aerobic state.

Given the advantages and disadvantages of anaerobic composting described in the prior paragraph, if you can wait for your compost and have enough space that any smell won't have your neighbors showing up with pitchforks and torches, you can save yourself a lot of work. If you have a garage or porch that doesn't freeze in winter and you can endure the smell, you can even make anaerobic compost in the house.

The principles of anaerobic composting are straightforward. Place organic matter in a mass and keep oxygen from reaching it to any substantial degree. If you leave it long enough it will turn into compost. In practice, anaerobic composting takes place in two phases: an anaerobic phase in which it is extremely damp or even completely submerged in water and an aerobic phase in which the excess water is allowed to evaporate so it can finish curing and be used.

If you recall the first chapter of this book, I stated that you shouldn't worry too much because even if you mess up, you'll still make compost. Well, you can think of anaerobic compost as aerobic composting in which you did everything wrong . . . and it still worked.

Anything that can be composted aerobically can also be composted anaerobically. However, the carbon/nitrogen ratio for anaerobic compost should ideally be 25 or lower, which means the optimum ingredients are a bit different than in aerobic compost. You are best to avoid things like wood chips, sawdust, dried hay and dead leaves in anything but very small quantities because the C/N ratio that is optimal for anaerobic composting is much lower than for other types of composting, and these sorts of items have a lot of carbon.

Anaerobic Microbes

Anaerobic composting gets off to a slow start as the carbohydrates, fats and proteins are broken down via hydrolysis into simple sugars, fatty acids and amino acids respectively. These products are then acted upon by acidogenic and acetogenic bacteria to create a variety of organic acids and by-products including acetic acid. Methanogenic archaea[38] then finish the job by converting the acetic acid to methane. If you've read my book on fermenting, you know that acetic acid is the active ingredient in vinegar, and that vinegar is made by aerobic bacteria. That is true—when the vinegar is being made from alcohol. But the acetic acid in compost is made

---

38 Archaea are a classification of microorganism that are sufficiently similar to bacteria visually that they were only recently determined to constitute their own domain.

from organic acids, which require an anaerobic organism as the intermediary.

Without going too deeply into the chemistry, anaerobic microbes use electron receptors such as carbon monoxide or sulfate ions in place of oxygen in their metabolism. You can find them peacefully composting organic matter in silt at the bottom of lakes, in our digestive tracts as friends, and lurking at the end of rusty nails as foes. Certain anaerobic archaea are called extremophiles because they can be found in places such as boiling hot natural springs, acid run-off from strip mines and other places normally inhospitable for microbes.

Though anaerobes produce some carbon dioxide as a product of metabolism, just as do aerobic bacteria, their primary respiratory by-product in a digester is methane. They also produce smelly gases such as hydrogen sulfide (think of rotten eggs) and ammonia. By-products of anaerobic composting that has not yet completed often contain the same compounds that give animal corpses a foul smell such as putrescine and cadaverine, as well as compounds such as skatole and indole that give feces their distinctive odor. Thankfully, these have dissipated by the time the compost is ready, but during composting they may assault your senses.

The aggregate gas created through anaerobic composting is called marsh gas, and it contains sufficient methane[39] to be a power source if you are making enough anaerobic compost for harvesting the methane to be practical.

---

39 Methane is the primary flammable material found in natural gas. It is also one of the primary gases in the atmosphere of Jupiter. Lake Kivu in the Democratic Republic of Congo contains 72 billion cubic yards of methane dissolved in the water, and it explodes on a millenial scale causing extinction events in its vicinity.

Anaerobic microbes can be divided into two broad classes: facultative anaerobes that will work either with or without oxygen and obligate anaerobes that will either die or stop growing if they are exposed to oxygen.

Obligate anaerobes find their way into compost because many of them form spores upon exposure to oxygen. Their spoors remain inert and intact until placed in conditions favorable for their emergence and multiplication. This is how tetanus and botulism, both obligate anaerobes, survive.

The most important consideration with anaerobes is that they don't like oxygen. Once you have sealed them off from oxygen, they should remain so until enough time has passed to allow for complete composting. Exposing them to oxygen will kill or disable microbes that won't be able to get back to work until the oxygen you introduced has again been depleted.

Though all living or once-living materials contain spoors for anaerobic bacteria suitable for composting, the quantity present is pretty small. Your first batch of anaerobic compost may take a while to get started just because it will take some time for the bacteria to multiply sufficiently. After this, just save some finished compost from each batch, and mix in a shovelful with subsequent batches. This will inoculate them and get them off to a faster start.

Overview of Anaerobic Techniques

By convention, any device intended to contain anaerobic compost is called a "digester" and the anaerobic composting process is often called "fermentation". The principles and practice of anaerobic composting can be carried out in an infinite variety of ways. The key is to exclude oxygen and have an appropriate C/N ratio of less than 25.

One thing to keep in mind is that the C/N preference of 25 is based on the fact that materials with lower C/N ratios usually contain sufficient moisture to support composting in and of themselves and will result in finished compost more quickly. But if you don't mind adding enough water to the digester to exclude oxygen spaces, even compost with a C/N ratio as high as 40 will work just fine.

Digesters can be divided into two categories: dry digesters, and wet digesters. Dry digesters aren't exactly dry. Ingredients that already have a high level of moisture are chopped and sealed in the digester. As fermentation proceeds, water is expelled from the materials creating sufficient moisture. By the time fermentation has completed, that water has been consumed in the metabolic processes of the microbes. You can add water to the ingredients in a dry digester before sealing it if the ingredients have insufficient moisture.

Wet digesters are like a septic tank in that the materials are submerged in water to protect them from oxygen. Because a lot of the generated gases are absorbed into the water, these tend to be less smelly than other methods, but only until the water is disturbed and the dissolved gases are liberated.

Open Pile Anaerobic Composting

In an open pile, oxygen is excluded by incorporating enough water to fill all the air pockets. Between 45 and 70 percent water is required, but usually it is closer to the 70 percent. As successive layers are added to the pile, water is added to each layer and the pile is covered with a water proof barrier such as a plastic tarp to keep water from evaporating quickly. As each new layer is added, that layer is watered thoroughly and the tarp is re-installed.

Once the pile is as large as you want it, you stop adding new materials. Every once in a while the tarp is removed and the pile is thoroughly watered until it won't accept any more water, then the tarp is put back on.

The compost will be ready in a year. Yes, it's a long time and we're impatient by nature. But it is also the least labor-intensive way of making compost.

In practice, the top couple of inches of the compost won't compost because of excess oxygen or insufficient water. Once the primary composting has completed and you've removed the tarp, just mix it thoroughly and treat it like mesophilic aerobic compost and it will be ready in a couple of months.

Anaerobic Container Composting

You can make an anaerobic composter out of a large trash container. Cut a 1'-diameter hole in the bottom, set it into a small flat space you have dug in the yard to fit, shovel dirt back around the outside edges to exclude air, and then fill it with thoroughly-watered organic matter, making sure to close the lid tightly. Keep filling the container until nothing more will fit.

You can make a small version of this with a 5-gallon bucket and a sealing lid. Drill a number of 1/2" to 1" holes in the bottom to allow contact with soil as it sits in the earth. Just as with using an open pile, let it sit for a year after your last addition and you'll have finished compost. Because it is tightly sealed, it won't have the same problems with the top layer as with the open pile method.

One advantage of this method is that the containers have an open bottom buried in the earth, so that when the compost is ready, earth worms will move in and further enrich the compost.

Though it is a bit less efficient because it doesn't completely exclude oxygen, you can re-task one of the containers sold as enclosed composting bins. These make really poor aerobic composters which is why I don't recommend them for the purpose, but if you seal the vents with duct tape, they will work pretty well anaerobically, except you'll need to add water periodically.

Buried Composting

So long as you are using materials that don't contain feces (because of the E. coli risk), you can practice buried composting in a fallow garden bed or other spot. In the spring, once the ground is workable, dig a trench between a foot and a half and two feet deep. Throw in your materials, tightly packed, and then cover with soil for six inches. Sow with a cover crop, and the next spring it will have composted and will enhance your soil's fertility.

How large a space you use for this will depend on how much material you have, but you want at least enough material to be a foot deep in the bottom of the trench. Over time, that material will take up less space so save the excess soil you excavated to fill in the trench the next spring. Composting in this fashion gives results that are nothing short of amazing.

Garbage Bag Composting

The lowly garbage bag is an unusual but quite workable composting solution that lends itself to composting indoors.

Add the materials, most often kitchen waste, to a large garbage bag until you have at least twenty pounds of material. Make sure it is sufficiently wet, and then completely seal the bag. Put that bag inside another one, and seal the outside bag as well. Then put it somewhere in the home where it won't freeze and you won't accidentally step on it. After a year, come back and you'll have finished compost.

The most important thing is to avoid puncturing the bags because during the composting process a lot of water is squeezed from the materials and if the bags are punctured the fluid that leaks out will be really vile—especially for the first couple of months. This same technique can be used with anything that seals tightly.

Garbage bag anaerobic compost is the perfect way to have compost ready in the spring for making seed starting mixes and soil block recipes. Where I live, sometimes the ground is frozen well into April, and as my compost piles are in the shade my finished compost is still covered with snow, hard as a brick and inaccessible. I need compost as early as January for starting my onion seedlings in soil blocks, and garbage bag anaerobic compost is the easiest solution imaginable.

Septic Style Composting

Covering compost ingredients with water excludes oxygen completely, guaranteeing anaerobic conditions. This can be done as easily as adding your materials to a barrel and covering with water as needed. Once the barrel is full and all ingredients are fully submerged, stop adding ingredients. Because the water protects the materials from oxygen, a lid isn't strictly necessary, but I recommend a loose-fitting lid just to keep rain from causing the barrel to overflow. Every so often, check and make sure to add water if the water level is getting too low.

I recommend a barrel of around twenty-gallon capacity because it is more easily handled than larger barrels and retains more heat than small buckets. You can make your own wet anaerobic digester for about $27[40] as follows.

Wet Anaerobic Digester

Materials

- 1 × 20 gallon dark-colored, flat-bottomed outdoor plastic garbage can with lid
- 1 × 1/2" threaded to glued PVC adapter
- 1 × 1/2" PVC threaded coupling
- 1 × Tube silicone
- 1 × PVC ball valve
- 1 × 4" piece of 1/2" PVC pipe
- 1 × 8" piece of 1/2" PVC pipe
- 1 × PVC cement

Procedure

1. Drill a 3/4" hole in the side of the garbage can between halfway and two-thirds of the way from the bottom.

⊗ I used a 3/4" spade bit gently to make the hole.

---

40 Using 2012 prices at a chain home improvement store, prices were: garbage can, $13; adapter, $1.20; coupling, $1.20; ball valve, $2.70; silicone, $3; cement, $4; PVC pipe, $1

2. Screw the threaded end of the adapter through the hole.
3. Apply a generous amount of silicone around the inside and outside of the adapter.
4. Screw the coupling onto the adapter.
5. Allow to cure for the requisite time specified by the tube of silicone.
6. Use PVC cement to attach the 4" and 8" pieces of PVC pipe to the PVC ball.
7. Use PVC cement to attach the unattached end of the 4" piece of pipe to the non-threaded end of the PVC adapter.
8. Turn off the ball valve and your digester is ready to use!

⊗ The silicone forms a seal so the digester won't leak.

⊗ The anaerobic digester is ready for use!

Wet anaerobic digestion takes place more slowly than dry methods because the temperature is lower. You can speed up the process by placing the barrel in a sunny place so the sun will lend warmth. Though most anaerobic composting takes place at mesophilic temperatures, the microbes involved (archaea) are adaptable to warmer environments. So putting the barrel in the sun will help speed up their metabolism. Because I live in a cold climate, a wet digester is only practical for me from May through September. I can fill the digester for the month of May, top it off and then forget it until September. When I check it in September, it is ready and I use the compost and effluent on my beds.

You'll know this process is done when it is stable. That is, if you give it a stir and the smell is simply like manure or dirt. If it smells like rotten eggs, ammonia, or something even worse, it isn't ready.

Once it is ready, the bottom of your digester will be covered with a six-inch to one-foot thick layer of brown sludge—this is your compost. But the water above it is rich in nutrients too, and if the compost is completely finished, it is an anaerobic compost extract that is ideal for watering transplants in the garden.

Getting the water out of the digester can be difficult, but it is a problem easily solved in advance by using a digester like the one described. Drain as much of the aqueous compost extract as you can via the PVC spigot. Once that much of the effluent has been drained, the digester is light enough that you can tip it to get the rest of the liquid out, and then scoop out the sludge with a shovel.

You can apply the sludge to your beds immediately or add it to maturing aerobic compost in your compost pile for further processing.

Caution

I discussed E. coli in a previous chapter but I want to emphasize this. In industry, wet composting is primarily used with animal manures, and the methane is recovered to produce energy. However, the anaerobic process doesn't effectively eliminate the E. coli that can be present in manures.

If animal manures or carcass parts are used in your ingredients for anaerobic compost, do NOT apply the effluent from wet digesters directly to your plants unless it is at least 120 days before harvest. Instead, use it to water a thermophilic compost pile so the nutrients will be retained and the thermophilic process will kill the E. coli.

The same goes for the sludge from a wet digester or the compost made via anaerobic methods. If it has vegan ingredients, no problem. But if it included animal manures or carcass parts, you should observe the same caution as with fresh manure and either apply it more than 120 days before the harvest of the crop or simply add it as an ingredient in a thermophilic pile.

6

Aerobic Composting

When people speak of compost, what they usually have in mind is compost that is made using aerobic methods. The reasons are simple. Aerobic compost may be more labor intensive to make, but it is completed more quickly than other methods—in as little as three months. Only aerobic composting has the potential to generate thermophilic temperatures that will directly kill all known human pathogens.[41] Aerobic composting, when done well, is nearly

---

41 With the exception of prions, but these are easily avoided as described in Chapter 3.

odor-free. The resulting compost can be used to make compost tea. It smells sweet and earthy. You can run your hands through it fearing at most a centipede.

The gist of aerobic composting is combining your materials in the correct C/N ratio, providing sufficient moisture but not too much, and keeping the pile aerated so it has plenty of oxygen. Aerobic composting can be done either thermophilically (hot pile) or mesophilically (ambient temperature pile).

You can choose whether your compost is mesophilic or thermophilic by the C/N ratio. A C/N ratio of 25–35, when the moisture level is correct and the pile is properly aerated, will result in thermophilic compost. If the C/N ratio is lower than 25 it can still be thermophilic, but only if considerable care is taken to disperse excess moisture from the pile through constant turning. A C/N ratio of 35–50, given proper aeration and moisture, will compost, albeit at the lower mesophilic temperatures. Piles with a C/N ratio greater than 50 will compost mesophilically . . . eventually. They lack the nitrogen needed by microbes to form their basic proteins, so they break down very slowly. For example, I have a pile of sawdust that has been sitting in my driveway for three years and you can still distinguish the individual chips. The C/N ratio of sawdust is over 100, so all by itself it breaks down slowly. If I were to mix it with some grass clippings and lower the C/N ratio, it would turn into compost in a flash.

You can also choose whether your compost is mesophilic or thermophilic by the volume of the pile. Imagine a box that is a perfect 1' cube. It has 6 sq. ft of surface area that will dissipate the heat contained within 1 cubic foot, so the ratio of surface area to volume is 6:1. Now imagine the same cube, only measuring 3' per side. Its volume is

27 cubic feet, and its surface area is 54 sq. ft, giving a ratio of surface area to volume of 54:27 or 2:1. This means that the smaller cube will dissipate a given amount of heat content three times better than the larger cube. Or to put it differently, the larger cube retains heat better than the smaller one. Though it is somewhat dependent on ambient temperature (because heat flows from a zone of higher heat to a zone of lower heat at a rate determined by their differential), overall the major factor in being able to sustain a thermophilic pile is the pile's size. You can have the C/N ratio, moisture level and oxygen absolutely perfect for thermophilic compost and if the pile isn't large enough it won't retain enough heat to reach thermophilic temperatures. In general, you want at least a cubic yard of compost though it can be done with as little as 12 cubic feet with careful management. Any lesser volume is going to be mesophilic unless done in a very well insulated box.

You can also control whether compost is thermophilic or mesophilic through the addition of cooling materials—specifically, the amount of garden soil or dirt you add. A shovel of soil is great to give compost piles a microbial boost, but if soil forms more than a minor amount of the mass of the pile, it will have a cooling effect. By the time soil makes up a quarter of the pile, it will be mesophilic no matter what other factors are present. During the thermophilic phase of compost, you don't want the temperature going higher than 160°F (as measured with a soil/compost thermometer). If it does, you can add a bit of soil to each layer as you turn it, and it will cool down a bit while still remaining in the thermophilic range.

So why would it matter whether your compost is mesophilic or thermophilic? There are benefits and detriments to each. Thermophilic composting has the benefit of killing pathogens and breaking down organic materials so quickly and effectively that you can compost practically anything, including livestock carcasses, manures and even human waste safely and in short order. For typical garden use, if you give it close attention and turn/water/adjust as needed, you can have finished and cured compost in three months. On the downside, it requires frequent turning and its sheer rapidity causes the loss of about half of the nitrogen in the pile in the form of ammonia.

Mesophilic compost, because it isn't processing as quickly, doesn't need to be turned as often. It still needs turning, and you should still watch the moisture levels, but you can get away with turning a mesophilic pile once a month or so, as opposed to thermophilic piles, which need turning sometimes every day or every other day during their thermophilic phase. It takes longer to be finished and cured, usually from nine to twelve months. On the other hand, it retains nearly all of the nitrogen with very little having been lost into the atmosphere.

Thermophilic aerobic composting takes place in three distinct phases:

Mesophilic Phase

Mesophilic composting will occur without regard to C/N ratio if your pile isn't big enough to maintain adequate heat for thermophilic composting, or when the C/N ratio is much higher than 30, because of the limited nitrogen supplies for bacterial reproduction. But even a pile built to be thermophilic with everything done perfectly will start off with a short mesophilic phase lasting a couple of days. During this time, mesophilic organisms start breaking down materials and making them juicy. As they progress, the pile heats up. Once the temperature exceeds about 100°F the mesophilic organisms take a break. If the pile is designed to be mesophilic, this phase is quite prolonged and the next (thermophilic) stage is skipped.

Thermophilic Phase

As the mesophilic organisms back off, thermophilic organisms step into the gap and really get things going with temperatures rising to as high as 160°F Depending on the size of the pile and its ingredients, the thermophilic phase may last anywhere from several days to several months, and it will shrink substantially.

You may wish to skip the thermophilic phase in order to retain more nitrogen. Though the difference in retained nitrogen is small, it can be important if you are on a frontier where obtaining outside sources of nitrogen is difficult or impossible. To do this, mix one part of garden soil for every four parts of compost ingredients into your pile. This will cool your pile down. Remember that mesophilic compost takes longer to cure to readiness.

Maturing and Curing Phase

As the thermophilic phase or the extended mesophilic phase runs out of food, the pile will cool down and mesophilic organisms will become active again, followed by actinomycetes and fungi. Finally, multicellular organisms such as earthworms will find a home, telling you the compost is ready.

Ingredients

Anything that was once alive can be added to aerobic compost. If you're like me, you've read many articles about composting, and nearly all of them written for the casual reader admonish that you shouldn't add cooking oils, meat or any animal materials to your compost pile. Somehow, somewhere, some expert said this, and everyone has repeated it ever since.

The real concern with including animal parts, meat and cooking oil in compost is attracting predators and scavengers to your pile. I've been told that I live pretty much in the middle of nowhere. My yard has seen bears, deer, foxes, coyotes, raccoons, opossums and all manner of other animals. I have never had a problem with animals digging into my compost pile to get at animal materials because when I add them, I dig a hole in the pile a couple of feet deep, add the materials, and then cover them with compost. That covering material creates a biofilter that contains any odors, so scavengers aren't attracted. I do the same thing with eggs. (Make sure you break eggs when you add them so they are fully processed.)

Large-scale agriculture has been composting animal remains for years in order to reduce pollution of rivers and streams. It is perfectly safe so long as it is done thermophilically. According to the University of Georgia College of Agriculture and Environmental Sciences: "The composting process converts dead birds into a useful, inoffensive, stable end product that can be field-applied for crop use and soil improvement." It states that: "Fly larvae, pathogenic bacteria and viruses are destroyed through the combined effects of time and temperature during composting. Typical temperatures achieved during composting exceed the human waste treatment requirements of the Environmental Protection Agency (130°F for fifteen days)."[42]

The last quote brings up another matter: human waste. We can call it urine and feces, or we can call it excrement. Within the context of composting, it is called humanure. And yes, it can indeed be safely composted using aerobic thermophilic methods. Most likely you have a regular toilet, as do I. But, for emergencies that result in a lack of power or water, I have a composting toilet.

Though I only use humanure compost for landscaping and not for crops, that is strictly due to the fact that I may wish to pursue organic certifications for selling produce, because it is entirely safe.[43] I'll speak more of composting toilets later.

All other likely ingredients in compost are not controversial. You can use anything that was once alive or that is produced by something that is alive. Refer back to Chapter 2 for the table of C/N ratios and an explanation of how to achieve a particular desired ratio. You want to aim for a C/N ratio of 25–30 for thermophilic compost, and if you are processing animal materials or manures, you must use thermophilic composting to make it safe. With a higher C/N ratio, as high as 50, your pile will be mesophilic. If your C/N ratio is above

---

42 Worley, J. and Ritz, C., *Poultry Mortality Composting Management Guide* (Georgia: CAES, 2012).
43 Although the EPA has standards for composting human waste, the National Organic Program does not allow human waste in any form. If you are looking for USDA Organic or Certified Naturally Grown certification, you cannot use humanure compost on crops whether it is safe or not.

50, it will take approximately forever or as long as two or three years to be ready.

When making compost, you want as diverse a pool of ingredients as you have available. In my piles, the primary ingredients are leaves that have fallen from trees in the fall, grass clippings, crop debris, cuttings and cover crops from the garden. But when I have a chance to go to the beach, I haul back a few five-gallon buckets of seaweed; I put my poultry manure and processed chicken carcasses in the pile as well as kitchen scraps, weeds, the dross from making beer and wine, aged sawdust from cutting trees and so forth. I have even gone down to a local river and filled up a bucket with river water to pour on my pile. By using as many different ingredients as you can, you end up with compost that is rich in micro-nutrients that will super-charge your garden.

Moisture

Aerobic compost is a bit touchy regarding moisture. There has to be moisture to supply the bodily functions of microbes, but not so much that it drives out the air that they need. Most guidelines give a range of 45 percent to 60 percent water by weight. That's pretty good advice for industrial composting, but I'm not sure it's very helpful for those of us who can't seem to fit our compost piles on a scale. My bathroom scale goes up to 300 pounds, but I estimate my largest compost pile at a couple of tons and hauling it into the house wouldn't be easy.

Instead, pick up a clump in your hands and try to squeeze it. If it is moist enough to stay together but not so moist that water runs out, you've got it right. If you find the idea of sticking your hands into unfinished compost less than appealing, you can pick up some disposable latex or polyurethane gloves in the cleaning aisle at the supermarket. Early in the composting process, even this sort of test might not work very well because the various constituents of the composting mass are too large. In that case, just feel it. Is it damp? Good. Is it wet/soggy? Bad. Is it dry? Bad. That's really all there is to it.

If your pile is too damp, you can add other materials, but the simple act of turning the compost will help. If it is too dry, the next time you turn it, spray it down thoroughly with a water hose after every six inches or so.

The water in a compost pile is being used up continuously. Some of it evaporates from the pile, but a lot of it is used in biological processes. So whenever you turn the pile, check the moisture and add some water if it is needed.

Aeration and Turning

When you are first building your pile, aeration is achieved by layering ingredients to provide air space (an example would be putting a layer of corn stalks between layers of leaves and grass clippings) and by using a containment system that allows air to enter. Materials used for making air spaces will break down over time and the oxygen in those gaps will be consumed. Eventually you'll need to turn the pile to get oxygen back into it.

Turning a compost pile is an absolutely back-breaking chore. There's no point in

⊗ Turning compost with a shovel is excellent whole-body exercise.

lying to you about this while writing odes to the loveliness of compost. There is no such thing as a free lunch anywhere in nature, and aerobic compost is no exception. If you want it, you are going to have to work for it! However, because so many of us have sedentary jobs, the labor—though difficult—is also good whole-body exercise! I use a digging fork for compost that hasn't broken down much because the sharp tines just get right in. In later phases, I use a shovel. I'll show you my bin system shortly, but what I do is shovel or fork over all the compost from one bin into another. This puts the top on the bottom, the outside to the inside and aerates thoroughly.

There are, of course, other ways to aerate compost. But since there is no free lunch, every method is going to require either additional equipment (meaning extra money) or extra time.

One way is to insert PVC tubes with hundreds of holes drilled into them vertically into the pile. You can also make a manifold of such tubes with horizontal inter-connecting pieces. Because of the need to bring outer materials back to the inside for complete composting, such a system won't prevent all necessity of turning, but it can reduce the need by about half. You'll still need to turn the compost to check and add water, and so forth.

There are a couple of companies that make large drums for containing compost. The drums will turn your compost automatically because they are on a rotating system that allows you to turn your compost by giving it a crank or a spin. It's a good idea and it works beautifully. The downside is that they are expensive, seldom locally available, and cost a fortune to ship. Furthermore, they barely hold a yard and a half of compost which is enough to go thermophilic, but at least in my case the capacity is insufficient so I'd need several of them. However, if you are flush with cash and your compost operations are small, getting a couple of these (so the compost can age in one while the other is being filled and turned) would work fine and make compost with little effort. I like this idea well enough that I have integrated it into a small-scale mesophilic indoor composting system that I describe in the next chapter.

Another alternative is to use a garden auger that fits in a 3/8" drill. These come in various diameters and lengths, but you want one that has at least a 2" diameter and is at least 24" long so you can go as deeply into the pile as possible. As they come from the factory, they will turn in the drill chuck unless you grind a flat spot onto one side so they will hold. I use mine with a plug-in drill rather than

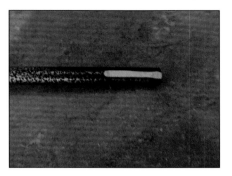

❂ Grind one part of the auger flat or it will turn in the drill chuck.

❂ A garden auger will save your back but requires patience.

❂ This harpoon-type compost aerator works better on coarser compost than on my nearly-finished compost.

a cordless so it has plenty of power. A garden auger helps grind up and mix the compost while aerating, and you can avoid heavy lifting. Remember that there is no such thing as a free lunch? If your compost pile is very big, this is pretty time consuming. Figure about an hour for a 3" × 3" × 3" pile.

There are also various designs of compost aerators. Some are spirals that you turn, and others are like harpoons that you plunge into the pile and then pull back out. The thing to keep in mind is that none of these will effectively bring the outside of the pile into the inside of the pile, so you will still need to get a shovel or digging fork at least once. I have tested some of the harpoon-style compost aerators and though they are better than a sharp stick in the eye, they aren't *much* better. Your mileage may vary, so don't let me discourage you if you want to try them out.

One other resource bears mentioning: teenagers. Teenagers make excellent manual laborers if properly motivated with cash. The last time I had a few tons of compost that needed shoveling, I paid two teens to do the job and they polished it off in a couple of hours. It's good for them and gets them away from the video game controller.

How often should a pile be turned? During the thermophilic phase, it should be monitored with a compost thermometer and turned whenever the temperature starts to drop. After a day or two, it will heat back up again. This process is continued until the pile no longer reaches temperatures higher than 130°F. During a longer mesophilic or curing phase, the pile should be turned anytime it has noticeably shrunk, requires the addition of water, or at least monthly.

The Process in a Nutshell

Add materials to your compost bin either as a large batch or incrementally as they become available. Don't worry too much about turning until the pile is as large as you'd like, though it will shrink a bit. Once the pile is as large as you'd like, at least twenty-seven cubic feet, turn it for the first time.

As you turn the pile, observe. Is it smelly? If so—is it also very wet? If that is the case, add some material with a C/N ratio higher than 30 to the layers of the pile as you shovel it over. Good choices would be wood chips, dry leaves or sawdust. If it is smelly but is not very wet, check the moisture. If it needs water, add some to each layer as you shovel it over. Likely, it is insufficiently aerated and shoveling will do the trick. If the materials have adequate moisture, aren't very smelly but don't seem to be breaking down at all, then the nitrogen is too low.

Within a couple of days, your pile should heat up. Use a compost or soil thermometer to check the temperature between nine and twelve inches under the surface of the compost. Give it another couple of days if it hasn't heated up. If, by the fifth to seventh day your compost hasn't reached at least 130°F, something basic is wrong. Either the moisture is wrong, the C/N ratio is too high or it is insufficiently aerated. Shovel it over again. If it is smelling like a sewer or like feces, then its C/N ratio is too low or there is too much moisture. If the moisture level is okay, add something carbonaceous such as some sawdust as you shovel it over. If it is smelling okay and the moisture level is okay, then the C/N ratio is too high. You can add alfalfa, blood meal, grass clippings or any number of other substances with a low C/N ratio to each layer as you shovel it over. Within five days your compost thermometer will show at least 130°F.

During this thermophilic phase, monitor the temperature daily. Once the temperature has dropped below 130°F, turn the compost again. As you turn it, check the moisture level and add water as needed. Now that it has been turned, the compost should heat up again within a day or two. Continue this process until the compost will no longer reach a temperature fifteen or more degrees higher than the ambient air temperature. Now, you enter the maturing and curing phase.

During the maturing phase, you can turn your compost a couple of times at your convenience, any time the pile has noticeably shrunk or anytime it needs water. After a while everything from worms to mice will make homes in it. Before you use it, check to see that it has matured.

How to Check Compost Maturity

Immature compost generates compounds that prevent seed germination, and it will tend to rob nitrogen from the soil (as it tries to to complete itself once you've added it to your garden). Neither is a good thing.

The maturity of compost can be visually evident if you start seeing weeds growing out of the pile and note the presence of plenty of earthworms. These both tell you the compost is ready.

⊗ This earthworm and its friends report that the compost is ready.

Another test you can do is the radish seed test. Radish seeds are especially sensitive to the compounds in immature compost that inhibit germination, so they are an easy way to test. Get two flats. In the first flat, put in seed starting mix. In the second flat, use a mixture of 75 percent seed starting mix with 25 percent compost. Plant fifty seeds in each flat and keep damp. After most of the seeds in the first flat have germinated, check the germination in the second flat as well. If the germination in the second flat is at least 80 percent of what it is in the first flat, then your compost is finished.

There are also expensive commercial tests for compost maturity. These make sense on an industrial scale where compost doesn't have contact with earth so the visual signs of completion won't be present, and where time is money and doing a germination test takes time. I don't recommend these because in your own garden you have the luxury of nature and your own time.

Where to Put Your Piles

In the shade. It's a shame to have a three-word answer for a five-word question, but that is really the gist of it. Some believe that putting a compost pile in the sun is helpful because the sun will help warm it up. It is true that, in general, biological and chemical processes are accelerated through the application of external heat, but the heat in a compost pile is generated by microbes from within, and the moisture loss from direct sun could actually hurt the pile.

So if you have an option, put your piles in the most shady spot on your property. If you have no shady spots, during the warmer months you'll need to water your pile. Just stick your finger in the top and if it is dry, water it.

Another option is to spread a tarp over it for shade, but you'd have to keep it at least a couple of feet from the pile to avoid the tarp creating a greenhouse and cooking your compost.

Compost Bins, the Easy Way: With Chicken Wire

I have seen a lot of articles describing bins of varying degrees of complexity. Some of them are real masterpieces, and others are just stacked up hay bales. Hay bales are awkward to carry and weigh at least forty-five pounds, and compost bins made of wood will ultimately rot so I wouldn't want to invest much effort in them.

What I do instead is make my compost bins out of chicken wire. Chicken wire is inexpensive in 50" and 100" rolls. As long as you wear gloves it is easy to work with and lasts for years and years. You can pound the posts into the ground anywhere it is convenient using a post driver, make your bins any size that you would like and move them anytime.

The posts come in two strengths, and I encourage you to get the stronger of the two. Each bin requires four stakes, though if you locate

⊗ The post driver makes quick work of fence posts and builds functional strength.

more than one bin side-by-side the bins can share two of the stakes, so that two bins will require six stakes and three bins will only need eight stakes. Get stakes that are 4' tall. Spray the top of the stakes with yellow paint so they are clearly visible and you don't run into them accidentally (their green color camouflages them). You can get chicken wire in various heights. The 48" tall chicken wire is best.

⊗ Paint the tops of your posts bright yellow to prevent injuries.

You may find that the smallish compost ingredients fall out through the holes in the chicken wire, but in practice I haven't run into any trouble with that. A little bit falls out, but compared to the bulk of the compost it is no big deal. Another downside is that pounding in the posts can require a bit of strength. When I first tried this system, I would start off standing on a ladder and using a sledgehammer in order to get the stakes into the ground, but then I discovered a post driver for posts and have lived happily ever after.

A post driver is a 17–25 lb hollow tube that has handles on the sides and is enclosed on the top. To install a fence post, you slide it over the top of the post, and merely slide it up, then slam it down. It installs fence posts in short order, and like shoveling compost, it makes for excellent whole-body exercise.

Additives

Every once in a while I get questions about compost additives. Though I am sure the companies that make these additives truly believe in their products and stand behind them, the simple fact of the matter is that they are unnecessary. Given the right conditions, everything in nature carries and supports the microbes that will return its nutrients to the earth. If you want a truly excellent starter, just spread a shovel full of rich garden dirt or finished compost from your last batch on the pile.

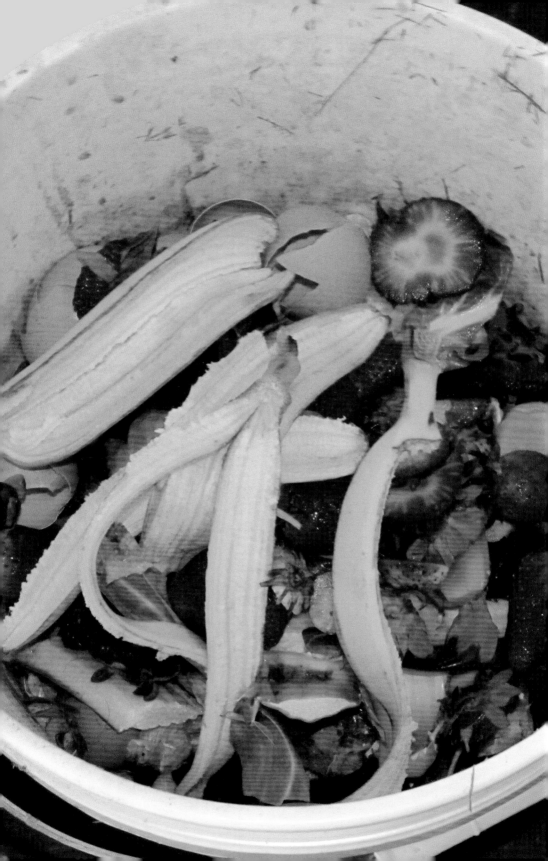

7

Indoor Mesophilic Composting

Like many gardeners, you may have ambitions to compost your kitchen waste. The trouble is that it is a royal pain to carry the stuff to an outdoor compost pile every time you make and eat a meal. Where I live, everything is frozen solid for four (or more) months out of the year anyway, so you can't dump stuff outside.

A lot of folk try putting their kitchen waste into a bucket that will be emptied into the compost pile periodically, but in many cases it becomes a smelly disgusting mess in less than a day. Putting a lid on top that will suppress the smell only makes the task of opening it difficult and the smell when it is opened even worse. And there is still the problem of wading through three feet of snow to a frozen compost pile Can you tell I speak from experience?

The problem is caused by the fact that kitchen wastes tend to have a C/N ratio of less than 30, plus supply so much moisture that when they start to break down, the contents of the bucket turn anaerobic within hours. The smell attracts flies, and pretty soon you just want the bucket gone.

Luckily, the nature of the problem itself specifies a couple of solutions. I discussed the first solution in the chapter on anaerobic composting: anaerobic composting in double-sealed trash bags. The other solution is to boost the carbon content of the compost, soak up the excess water and aerate the mass. The result is compost with greatly diminished (albeit not completely eliminated) smell. And you can do it indoors in the winter!

To that end, I have designed an indoor composting system based on three five-gallon buckets and a small stand that allows for easy bucket rotation for aeration purposes. The sequence of events is as follows:

- Fruit and vegetable wastes are put into the drum composter. For every pound of waste added, also add an absorbent carbon source as described later. Cut things up small. If you throw in a whole plum or a whole banana, you will attract fruit flies and generate unpleasant smells. *Small pieces are the secret to reducing odor in this system.*
- Rotate the drum at least five times daily. Leave the door facing upwards each time.

- Continue depositing waste and spinning until the drum is one quarter full. Then remove that drum from the cradle, put the second drum on the cradle in its place, and start adding materials to the second drum. Once or twice a day, put the first drum back on the rack and give it a spin for aeration. Check it once in a while to see if you need to add any moisture.
- After the first drum has gone a week with no new additions and daily aeration spins, empty it into the third bucket, and cover with a screen.
- Repeat.
- As each new addition is made to the third bucket, give the compost in the third bucket a stir.
- Once the bucket is full, leave it covered with the screen for a week then empty it into a large trash barrel. Don't cover the barrel. As you make new additions to the barrel, give them a stir. Your compost ages here.
- Use your compost in the fashion of ordinary compost after testing it for maturity.
- Note: the contents of the third bucket make great bedding for vermicomposting.

This system certainly works, but it is not without its flaws. While the bucket is being initially filled and for the first week of being tumbled without new additions, it will have some smell—though nothing as bad as a standard compost bucket. Because of that smell, it will also attract fruit flies. After the first week of being tumbled without new additions, though, there will be no noticeable smell and any fruit flies will be confined within it.

Indoor Mesophilic Compost Ingredients

Because this system is indoors and mesophilic, there are some restrictions on ingredients that wouldn't apply to an outdoor or thermophilic pile. You should avoid anything but incidental traces of meats, greases and oils. In substantial quantity, these would generate an impressive stench, attracting rodents. Also, although it might be tempting to empty the litter box into the compost barrel, this form of composting will not eliminate the eggs of the worms that infest so many cats nor the organisms transmitting toxoplasmosis. No animal feces of any sort should be used.

Barring those two restrictions, anything else you'd usually compost will work fine so long as it is properly prepared and mixed. So this doesn't completely solve the problem of composting all kitchen waste, but it deals with the fruits and vegetables that tend to be the most bulky.

The finer something is chopped, the better it works because it combines with the carbon more quickly to eliminate smells. So don't just dump a complete rotten cantaloupe in there. Instead, cube it before you put it in. The same applies for anything else. Instead of tossing in a whole carrot, chop it into chunks, etc. It works even better if you use a blender but that isn't necessary.

Carbon Sources

As I mentioned in the introduction, kitchen waste usually has a very low C/N ratio. In most cases, the C/N ratio averages 17 but it could be as low as 7 or as high as 35 depending on what was for dinner. But, on average, it is 17. Furthermore, as these materials break down they make a lot of moisture. All by themselves, the level of moisture is great enough to exclude oxygen and force the mass to become anaerobic.

Adding a carbon source serves the purpose of absorbing excess water and providing enough carbon to discourage anaerobic activity. Combined with aeration from turning the drum, materials should break down quickly with minimal offensive odor.

So what carbon sources should you use and how much should you add? There are a series of trade-offs with various materials. The more carbon you add, the less thermophilic the compost will be in its aerated state. Because the drums are small, they can't hold enough heat to compost thermophilically. But even without the high temperatures, the closer the final C/N ratio gets to 30, the faster breakdown will occur and the faster smells will be eliminated.

On the other hand, if the materials don't absorb enough moisture, the contents of the drum will stay anaerobic despite turning, and will stink. If the materials absorb too much moisture, the waste in the drum won't break down unless you add moisture. Since a major bonus of this method is the suitability of the end product for use in vermicomposting, I've identified four suitable carbon sources: peat moss, sawdust, shredded dry leaves and shredded newspaper.[44] I calculated the amount

---

44 When I speak of shredded newspaper, I am referring only to the news print, and NOT to the color glossies. I am also referring to newspaper that has been shredded with a paper shredder (available for $20 at an office supply store) as opposed to something you've torn up by hand.

to add based on an average resulting C/N ratio of 35. The closer you get the C/N ratio to 35, the more quickly any smells will abate.

- Sawdust: Add 0.25 lb (2 – 1/2 cup) per pound of kitchen waste. Nothing from pressure-treated lumber.
- Peat moss: Add 0.8 lb (3 – ¾ cup) per pound of kitchen waste. Any form of peat moss will do.
- Shredded newspaper: 0.25 lb (13 cup) per pound of kitchen waste.
- Shredded dry leaves: Add 0.7 lb (7 – 2/3 cup) per pound of kitchen waste.

In practice, I don't use just one of these materials. Instead, I keep two or three handy in pails near the composter and add a different material each time. This improved diversity of materials lets me use leaves when I am adding waste that doesn't need much absorption, peat moss when the waste is really watery, and news print when it is in between. What I have given above are guidelines, and are not written in stone. The most important thing is to add sufficient carbonaceous material to allow the compost to be damp but not wet. If sufficient material to achieve the right C/N ratio leaves your drum contents too dry, you can add water just as you would with an outdoor pile.

Making the Drums

The drums are made from standard five-gallon buckets. The handle is removed, the lid is affixed, a door is installed with rivets, and some holes are provided for aeration.

Materials for Each Drum

- 1 × 5-gallon pail with matching lid and seal
- 2 × hinges
- 1 × latch
- 3/16" aluminum pop rivets
- Foam weather stripping
- Talcum powder (do not substitute corn starch)

Procedure

1. Remove the handle.
2. Cut out a rectangular 4" × 6" hole. I used a saber saw.
3. Re-attach the rectangular piece using hinges and aluminum pop rivets.
4. Attach the latch to the bucket and rectangular piece.
5. With your door open, attach weather stripping so that it will form a seal with the door when it is closed.
6. Dust the exposed portions of the seal with talcum powder so it won't stick to the door when closed.
7. Directly opposite the door, drill a series of five

⊗ The important thing: proper alignment of the hole.

⊗ The hinges and latch attached with pop rivets.

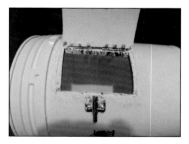

⊗ The drum with weather stripping installed.

1/8"–3/16" holes in a line lengthwise along the pail. These are for drainage.

8. Drill five additional 1/8"–3/16" holes at the cross quarters between the door and drainage holes. These are for aeration.

Making the Rotation Cradle

The rotation cradle is a platform that holds your compost drum on wheels so it can be easily rotated for aeration while providing a place underneath for a convenient container to catch any drips of moisture. It's a simple device consisting only of four short pieces of wood and four wheels spaced at the right distances to fit the drum.

Materials

- 2 2" × 4" lumber cut 15" long
- 2 2" × 4" lumber cut 12.5" long
- 8 3" #8 deck screws
- 4 Swivel casters with 2" wheels
- 6 1" #10 deck screws
- 1 Exterior latex or acrylic paint

❷ The lumber awaits our ministrations.

Procedure

1. Cut the lumber to the specified dimensions.
2. Lay the short pieces on the floor parallel to each other, edge side down.

❷ The joints are secured with deck screws.

⊗ The paint was a hardware store mistake, so I got it at half price.

⊗ You don't need casters this beefy, but they are what I had handy.

3. Lay the long pieces flat across the short pieces, even with the ends.
4. Secure each joint with two 3" #8 deck screws.
5. Paint the cradle with exterior latex or acrylic paint, and allow to dry.
6. Arrange the cradle in front of you with the longer pieces running left to right.

⊗ The completed drum and cradle. It spins nicely for easy aeration and mixing.

7. Place a mark 4" from the left end and 2" from the right on each long piece.
8. Arrange the casters evenly with the inner edge of each long piece, and inside each mark.
9. Secure each caster with four 1" #10 deck screws.
10. Your drum can now sit in the cradle and spin easily. Arrange the drum so the door is facing up and the drain side is facing down. Place a shallow open bin under the drum to catch any liquids.

Making the Bucket Screen

The bucket screen is nothing more than a lid for the bucket where you have cut out a hole to allow access to air and affixed a screen to discourage airborne invaders. If you don't want to make a special lid, you can use a large elastic or bungee cord to hold some screen in place over the top.

Materials

- 1 Sealing lid for bucket
- 1 6" × 6" piece of plastic window screen
- 1 hot melt glue stick

Procedure

1. Cut a 5" × 5" hole in the lid.
2. Turn the lid upside down, and use hot melt glue to attach the screen so it will cover the hole from inside.
3. Allow to harden.

8

Vermicomposting

Vermicomposting refers to the use of earthworms to convert waste, usually kitchen waste, into compost. In nature, you can tell when a compost pile is finished by the fact earthworms have made a home there. Earthworms improve the structure of soil via the nature of their excretions (called "castings"), and also improve its nutritional availability while adding to its microscopic life. They do wonders for the compost in your pile as well.

Vermicomposting is usually attempted as a way of composting indoors. Using standard techniques, people try to get earthworms to eat their kitchen waste directly. Lots of places sell special bins for the purpose as well as earthworms to stock the bins. It is better to be in the business of selling those bins than selling the resulting compost because most folk abandon their foray into vermicomposting within a couple of months due to various problems.

There is absolutely nothing wrong with the kits and if their instructions are followed to the letter, they work perfectly fine. The trouble is that trying to feed worms fresh food daily usually requires a lot more worm capacity than they have, and the result is rotting food, unpleasant smells and flies. I'll explain how this can be readily avoided so you can use those kits, or you can just make your own worm bins.

The Mighty Earthworm

In North America, particularly in the Northern sections, we have European explorers to thank for the fact that we have earthworms. The glacier advances across North America during the past couple of Ice Ages scraped off the topsoil and destroyed the earthworms already present. Thankfully, European explorers brought worms with them unintentionally in the soil supporting plants they imported and intentionally to improve the soils of their gardens. Across the region, roughly one-third of all worm species are imports from Europe, including night crawlers and red wigglers.

Invasive earthworms from Europe do occasionally cause problems, because the Northern forests evolved trees in their absence that depend upon a thick covering of leaves on the ground, and earthworms reliably turn these to humus. However, in our gardens, earthworms are an impressive asset.

Earthworms stimulate microbial activity, mix the soil, make soil clump better, provide channels for air and water, make nutrients more available to plants and shred plant residue. They take in anywhere from one-third to twice their body weight each day. Though small and toothless, their strong mouth muscles allow them to drag dead leaves and other detritus underground. Their castings contain more bacteria than they took in, and are encapsulated in mucus that helps aggregate the soil.

There are around 7,000 species of earthworm, though for our purposes they can be divided into three categories: those with deep burrows, those that live in the space between the topsoil and organic matter touching the soil, and those that live in topsoil. For purposes of composting, only the latter category is of interest because worms in the other two categories simply won't be productive or happy in a vermicomposting bin. Remaining species generally available are European night crawlers, African night crawlers and red wigglers. All three of these will consume at least their body weight in food daily, and will double their population every three or four months given friendly conditions. The most readily available and most widely recommended composting worm is the red wiggler. The one most to be avoided is the Canadian night crawler.

Anatomically, worms are essentially eating machines, with a digestive tract extending from the mouth at the front to the anus at the rear. (The front is the end nearest the bulge.) Though the digestive tract is a single uninterrupted tube, its various sections serve the purposes of a crop, stomach and intestines with peristalsis accomplished through banded and horizontal muscles. A rudimentary circulatory system runs between the alimentary canal and the skin, with oxygen being taken in from the skin's moist surface. If a worm's surface becomes too dry it won't be able to breathe and will die. Worms have some regenerative capacity, meaning that if a part is cut off, that part will regenerate, though the degree of regeneration depends upon where the worm was cut and the species of worm.

Though it isn't obvious, earthworms have appendages. Each segment has bristles called setae that can be extended or retracted. These serve as anchors, and the worm moves by anchoring some segments and stretching the others using its strong muscles. Worms cannot see, but their nervous system (which has several ganglia rather than a brain in charge) is connected to light sensitive cells on the surface. They also have chemical receptors that are similar to our senses of taste and smell.

Worms are hermaphroditic. That is, every worm has fully functional male and female parts. Some are capable of self-reproduction (parthenogenesis), but most require a mate. They mate by gluing themselves to each other with mucus, leaving a tube for the sperm to flow into the oviduct. After mating successfully, a worm will create a little lemon shaped cocoon about twice the size of a pin head containing both sperm and eggs. This cocoon is secreted from the raised band called the clitellum. All earthworms have one, though it is more obvious on some worms than others.[45] Depending on

---

45 Earthworms do not develop a clitellum until they are sexually mature, and when they get very old, they lose their clitellum. But all worms will have one through the majority of the worm life cycle. Most worms only live to be one or two years old, though some have lived from six to ten years.

species, the cocoon will hatch within two to four weeks, and the baby worms will emerge.

Your Worm Bin

A worm bin should be a place where worms are comfortable and happy. I have no idea how to directly assess a worm's psychological state, but the best measure is that the worms are eating their food, staying alive, and not trying to make a break for it. This can be best approximated by making a bin that duplicates their preferred natural environment as closely as possible.

Worms like moist but not wet soil that is well-aerated and rich in digestible organic matter. They have a serious aversion to light, and are highly sensitive to pesticides. They inhabit the top 6"–12" of soil, so a worm bin should be at least 6" deep but not more than 12" deep. Worms are most productive between temperatures of 55°F and 77°F, and will become inactive or die at temperatures below 32°F or above 85°F; so the worm bin should be in a location giving the best temperature range available in your home.

The length and width of the bin are a function of how much waste you are planning to compost. The rule of thumb is you need 1 sq. ft of worm bin surface area per pound of kitchen waste composted per week, but a minimum of 2 sq. ft. So for 1–2 lbs per week, select a bin that is 2 sq. ft, and to handle 5 lbs a week, select a bin that is 5 sq. ft.

This means that a worm bin should be opaque, covered to block light, be between 6" and 12" deep, present at least 2 sq. ft of surface area or 1 sq. ft per pound of waste weekly, and have provisions for aeration without harming the worms.

Because my kitchen waste is composted via a variety of methods, my worm bin is small. It is a large opaque storage container that I purchased at a discount store and filled with appropriate bedding material. I then set this into an identical bin for insulation. The top is covered with a plastic window screen to keep worms in and flies out, and the opaque top has some holes drilled in it for aeration.

Bedding

Worms need a place to sleep, live, eat and make babies. Like chickens, they also need a bit of grit for their crops to help them grind up food. They prefer moist bedding with a pH close to 7, which is neutral.

The most economical material is shredded newspaper. You can make all the shredded newspaper you could ever want with an inexpensive paper shredder purchased from a department or office supply store. Don't use the glossy inserts.

Because peat moss contains zero nutrients and therefore doesn't break down readily, you can't use it as the exclusive material for bedding. It has excellent qualities for holding and releasing moisture as needed, though, so you can use it for up to half your bedding material.

Another excellent material is compost that you have made indoors using the methods in the previous chapter. Don't use it for all of the bedding simply because it is so rich that the worms will be too busy eating it to eat your kitchen waste, but it will be good to use for up to a quarter of your bedding and its bacterial content will help get your worm bin off to a faster start. Compost from outside is NOT a good choice because it will definitely include a lot of creatures you don't want in the house even though most of them will be perfectly benign.

As I mentioned earlier, your worms need grit. Take a handful or two of garden soil, put it in a shallow container and go through it thoroughly removing any pebbles, plant matter, insects, larvae, other worms, etc. so that, to the naked eye, it is perfect soil. Put that in your worm bin and mix it with your bedding.

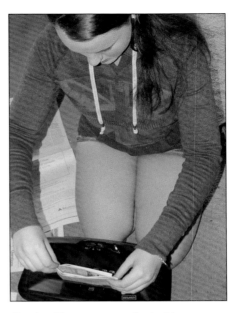

⊗ Shredding newspaper for bedding.

Your bedding needs to be very moist but not soaking wet. A general rule of thumb is you need three pounds of water for every pound of bedding. As a point of refer-

⊗ Damp bedding prepared from shredded newspaper, peat moss and a bit of clean dirt for grit.

ence, a pint of water weighs a pound. Put your bedding in a bucket, wet it until it is very moist but not dripping, mix in your soil for grit, and then put it all in your worm bin.

How Many Worms Do You Need?

I have heard it said that you can never be too rich, too thin, or have too many worms. Actually, I just made that up, and you really *can* be too thin. Even so, you'll need a lot of worms, though the precise quantity depends on exactly how you order them. I am assuming you'll be ordering red wigglers as they are the most readily available. Worms are sold as "pit run" meaning that worms of all ages are included, or as "breeders" meaning that the worms have been sorted so that only sexually mature worms are included. There are 1,000 breeders to

⊗ Worms newly introduced to the bedding.

a pound, though red wigglers sold as fishing bait are usually larger and thus there are about 600 per pound. A pound of pit run worms will include a lot of tiny babies, so the number is anyone's guess but could easily be more than 100,000.

Once your worm bin is well broken in with high bacterial levels, you should figure that worms will eat half their body weight daily, so if you make two pounds of waste daily, you'll need four pounds of worms. A pound of worms will eat 3.5 lbs of waste weekly. You will find suppliers of red wigglers through a search on the Internet or by calling your local Cooperative Extension Service.

To introduce your worms to the prepared bedding, gently pour them on top of the bedding and they'll burrow into the bedding as quickly as possible to get away from the light.

After half an hour, any worms still on top should be discarded because they are either sickly or dead. Once they've buried themselves, put the lid on to block the light.

What and How to Feed Your Worms

Worms don't eat your kitchen waste. Instead, they derive their nutrition from the microorganisms that grow on it as it breaks down. They don't have teeth, so they can't just chomp a carrot. Instead, what they'll do is suck on the portions that turn liquid as bacterial action breaks them down.

This is important information because it includes the secrets to successful vermicomposting: make your kitchen waste small by chopping or grinding, and bury it in the bedding. This way it will start breaking down faster and the worms will derive benefit more quickly. The second secret is that it takes a while for a vermicomposting bin to build up the optimal levels of bacteria, so start off with smaller feedings of about half or even a quarter of the planned capacity of your bin and build up slowly over a period of a few weeks. By the time you have built up to the full amount, your bin will be a veritable kitchen waste disposal machine with minimal smell.

But again, when you first start your bin there will be some smell and it will attract fruit flies because the worms eat the bacteria growing on your waste rather than the waste itself and it will take time for the bin to build up the requisite bacteria levels to rot the waste quickly. You can minimize the

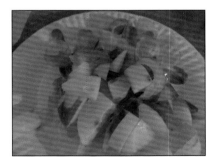

⊗ Cucumber peels and pieces are cut small for faster decomposition.

smell and fruit flies by burying waste rather than leaving it on the surface and by covering the top of the bin with a screen, but you should bury the waste anyway.

Divide your box using imaginary lines in your mind so that materials are buried under the surface of a different part of the

❷ The scraps are in the corner and will be buried to discourage fruit flies.

bin each time. It might take the worms a couple of days to get to it, but by the time you cycle back around to the first place you buried waste, it should be ready for new material.

Do not feed animal materials, meat or dairy. These are so high in nitrogen that with excess moisture they'll make the area immediately around them anaerobic and stink. Or if the moisture is absorbed and not excessive, it will make the area around them thermophilic and cook your worms. Save these items for the outdoor compost pile. You can certainly include what I describe as an incidental amount of meat. A bit of meat grease or butter covering some vegetables or a small piece of ground hamburger will do just fine. The key is to keep the amount small relative to other feed and your overall bin. You can't dump a pound of steak or a slab of cheese in there.

If you overfeed the worms, the bedding could turn acidic and hurt them. You'll know you are overfeeding if the bin starts to smell badly. Adequate food will encourage breeding, and inadequate food will slow breeding. If you need to take a vacation and can't feed your worms, they'll be fine for three weeks or so. If you'll be gone longer than that, you'll need a worm sitter to visit and feed them.

Unintended Critters

One day, you may notice creatures in your worm bin other than worms. Some of these are not a problem, but others are best avoided. The most likely unwelcome visitors will be fruit flies who have been attracted to the smells associated with the breakdown of fruits. You can avoid this by burying all scraps at least an inch below the bedding, and by limiting the amount of scraps you put in the bin so you don't exceed its capacity. If you are doing everything right and still attract fruit flies, you can get rid of them by placing a fruit fly trap nearby with a bait that is more attractive than your worm bin. Such traps are not 100 percent effective so in some cases you'll have to live with a few fruit flies. If you keep your bin covered with window screen to exclude the flies it will deny them a place to breed and keep their numbers in check.

You can buy fruit fly traps and baits, but you can make your own just fine. Take a soup bowl, fill it halfway full of fruit juice, beer or wine and add two drops of dish liquid and a tablespoon of vinegar. (The purpose of the dish liquid is to lower the surface tension of the water so the flies will sink rather than floating on top where they can crawl back up the sides.) Then, cover it with a piece of plastic wrap. Poke a few holes about the size of the tines on a fork in the plastic wrap. Fruit flies will enter but won't be able to find the exit.

Another potential pest is the fungus gnat. Fungus gnats eat all manner of decomposing material and once they are in your bin, getting rid of them won't be easy because what you are making in the bin is their dream food. Adding parasitic nematodes (steinernema feltiae) to the bin will control them effectively for a while because the nematodes will eat their eggs. Unfortunately, a parasitic nematode dies when it passes through the gut of an earthworm. So over time, the nematodes will lose effectiveness and you'll need to add them again if the fungus gnats return.

If you are seeing mice, rats, voles or moles, then in all likelihood you have included meat and dairy in your bin. The solution is to stop adding these materials and put the bin out of the reach of the rodents.

You may find millipedes in your worm bin. They eat waste and are perfectly harmless. They are usually brown or gray, round and long, with two pairs of legs per segment. They curl up into a ball or a spiral when disturbed. Because most millipedes that get into homes die from dehydration, they are attracted by the moisture in your compost. Once in the bin, they will help the worms along. They are nothing to worry about unless present in such numbers that they deprive worms of food.

Centipedes are another common worm bin visitor. These look dangerous and appropriately so, because they are predators who want to eat your worms! Centipedes in North America are usually brown to brownish-red with elongated and flattened bodies. They have one pair of legs per segment. All centipedes have a pair of poison claws behind their head which they use while hunting prey. Their claws are not usually

⊗ Centipedes are predators who want to eat your worms.

strong enough to penetrate human skin,[46] but if they do the result will include severe pain, swelling, fever and chills.[47] Centipedes are attracted to the worms as a source of food. Because centipedes are territorial, there won't be many in your worm bin. They can be eradicated by chasing them down and smashing them with a garden trowel or similar implement.

Mites are practically omnipresent so you'll undoubtedly have some in your bin. If populations get noticeable it will become a problem. The common white/brown mites eat the same food as earthworms, so though they don't pose a direct threat they could compromise the worms' food supply. Red mites, however, will suck the blood and juices out of earthworms and kill them. If you have a noticeable mite infestation, it is most certainly caused by the worm bin being too damp or by overfeeding. Let the bin dry a little, to the level of dampness needed in aerobic compost, and cut back on feed. Take the bin outside and put it in the sun with the top off for a couple of hours. That should take care of the mites.

Springtails, pot worms and sow bugs (commonly known as "roly poly" bugs) will likely find their way into your worm bin. Springtails range in size from that of a pinhead up to about a quarter of an inch. Their name is derived from a unique appendage present in most species of springtail. This appendage, called a furcula, is folded under the abdomen. When released, it propels them with a spring-like action.

---

46 Bush, Sean P. et al., "Centipede envenomation", *Wilderness & Environmental Medicine* 12 (2): 93–99

47 If you are allergic to bees, you may have an allergic reaction to centipedes as well. If you experience serious symptoms from any arthropod bite, seek medical assistance.

❸ Sow bugs are small crustaceans that are beneficial in your worm bin.

Springtails are harmless in the worm bin and help break down your waste. Pot worms are short white or nearly transparent worms. Like springtails, pot worms eat organic matter and aren't a problem. Sow bugs look like brown to gray mini armadillos. Some of them can coil up into a little ball, but most can't. They are tiny crustaceans with gills, and along with springtails are helpful allies in the worm bin and no cause for concern.

Another organism that is important to know about is mold. Mold is a natural aspect of a worm bin. Usually, it won't be obvious to the naked eye, but whether it is obvious or not it will most certainly be present as a vital aspect of vermicomposting. I mention this because some people are extremely sensitive to the presence of mold. If you or anyone in your family has a high sensitivity to mold, vermicomposting may not be a good idea. Not all molds are created equal, and though a person may have an allergy to "mold" they may not have an allergy to those molds present in the worm bin. But if you start a worm bin and shortly thereafter a family member develops problems related to mold allergy, you may not be able to keep a worm bin in your home.

Dividing Your Worm Herd

Worms can double their population in three or four months. At least, that's what everyone says. The reality is that their rate of reproduction is affected by prevailing temperatures and the amount of food available. When temperatures are lower, worms are less active, they won't eat as much, and they won't make as many babies. My bin sits on my enclosed porch, and during the winter the average temperature out there is about 60°F. At that temperature, they eat about half as much as usual and it takes them about six months to double their population. At temperatures under 55°F, they barely eat or reproduce at all. The same applies when temperatures exceed 84°F for a substantial period of time.

Without regard to their rate of reproduction, at some point when harvesting compost you'll likely decide you have way too many worms. When this happens, you can expand your vermicomposting operation by using a portion of your worms to start a new bin just as you did the first one. If you don't need to expand, you can repackage and sell the worms as fishing bait or to other folk interested in vermicomposting, or you can add them to a garden bed or a curing compost pile outside.

Harvesting Your Vermicompost

A properly sized bin will become rich dark compost in three to four months. When you are ready to harvest your compost, the largest task is to separate the worms and worm eggs from the compost. There aren't any 100 percent perfect ways, though some will work better than others.

Red wigglers aren't very big, and their castings are about the same diameter as their body, so just dumping the contents of your worm bin onto a screen won't work. A screen fine enough to hold back the worms and worm eggs would also hold back the compost.

Most methods of harvesting rely either on the worms' love of food or their aversion to light. When using either method, avoid feeding the worms for about ten days prior to harvest so that the compost won't have bits of food in it and so the worms will be hungry.

The light method is easiest. Put a bright light over your open worm bin for a few minutes. The worms will burrow deeper into the bin to avoid the light. Use a garden trowel and carefully scoop up the top inch of compost. Remove any worms or worm eggs from the compost you are scooping and put them back in the bin. As each layer is removed, the worms will burrow deeper. In practice, you'll only be able to repeat this process until you've harvested three-quarters of the compost, because the bottom quarter will be overcrowded with worms.

Leaving that compost behind will be helpful anyway because it will be a great source for the bacteria that breaks down kitchen waste and feeds worms. Once you have removed as much compost as you can, mix up some fresh bedding, dampen it appropriately and add it to the top of the worm bin and remove the light. The next day, start feeding your worms again.

The food method has about the same effectiveness. It relies on starving the worms for about ten days so they are good and hungry, putting an attractive food (such as melon rings or apple peelings) in one corner of the bin, waiting a day and a half to two days for the worms to all migrate to the food, and scooping out the compost starting with the corner furthest away from the food.

Another variant of this method is to put the attractive food into a mesh bag (such as the small laundry bags). You can bury this in one corner of the worm bin, wait a couple of days, and gently remove the bag full of worms and set it aside in a covered bucket while scooping out the compost. This allows for a bit more harvest than most approaches. As worms and worm eggs are encountered, put them in the bucket with the mesh bag.

You can return the worms to the bin by putting fresh damp bedding into your worm bin, and burying the mesh bag in one corner. Allow about three days for the worms to finish off their snack, and then bury food in the opposite corner. After a couple of days, you should be able to remove the mesh bag for re-use.

9

Composting Human Waste

I haven't seen human waste discussed in a garden-oriented composting book before, but because my readers generally have an interest in self-sufficiency, I believe the topic should be addressed. I understand the concern that human waste, having originated in humans, is the most likely medium for carrying human pathogens so there may be liability issues. I also understand that because of the risks posed by human waste there is a vast rubric of laws concerning its disposal. My advice could run afoul of laws so vast and different from locality to locality and state to state that anyone who followed the advice could get into trouble with the law. In fact, it would be impossible for any given piece of specific advice to be simultaneously compliant with laws across the country.

The trouble with looking at things from the standpoint of liability and legal compliance is that the subject of human waste is not addressed at all, and as a result people don't know what to do when confronted with situations in which the normal means of human waste disposal are unavailable. This could be the result of a long-term major power outage, terrorism or a natural disaster. In December of 2008, for example, an ice storm left many people in the Monadnock region of New Hampshire without access to electricity or running water for as long as a month. What are people in such circumstances supposed to do? Keep using their toilet even though it won't flush, with it stinking to the heavens and covered with flies?

So, with the understanding that compliance with laws is your responsibility rather than mine, and that this information could be used in circumstances where it is far superior to less sanitary alternatives, let's lift up the lid and dive into some human waste.

Why Is Urine Yellow and Why Are Feces Brown?

My grandfather once asked me to explain how a brown cow could eat green grass and make white milk. I was totally stumped, because I was all of six years old. When I asked why the manure was brown, he explained that the dirt in which the grass grew was brown, so it carried through into the manure.

His answer was intentionally fanciful, but these sessions with my grandfather naturally sparked my curiosity to find the real answers.

The more closely you examine the workings of the human body, the more amazing it becomes. Red blood cells in the human body have a life span of three or four months. Once they are too old to do their job, they are broken down in the spleen. Red cells contain a complex compound called hemoglobin that binds to oxygen in order to transfer it throughout the body. When the cells have reached senescence, the iron in the hemoglobin is retained for use in making new red blood cells and the rest of the compound is converted to bilirubin that is transferred to the liver. The body isn't wasteful. Though most of the bilirubin is secreted into the small intestine as part of bile, 95 percent of it is reabsorbed for re-use.

The remaining 5 percent makes it into the large intestine, where intestinal bacteria turn it into urobilinogen. Again, most of this urobilinogen is reabsorbed, and a small amount is eliminated by the kidneys as urobilin, which is what gives urine its yellow color. The urobilinogen that is not reabsorbed from the large intestine or eliminated by the kidneys is oxidized by bacteria to urobilin and stercobilin, the compounds that give feces their brown color.

Newborn babies are often put under sunlamps. The reason is because bilirubin is toxic to brain tissue, and the blood-brain barrier to keep bilirubin out of the brain is insufficiently developed in newborns. Their liver isn't working at full steam, and most importantly a newborn baby doesn't have any intestinal bacteria and therefore has no means of converting the bilirubin into urobilin or stercobilin so it can be eliminated from the body. The sunlamp changes the bilirubin into a more easily eliminated isomer. Combined with frequent feedings so that peristalsis is stimulated, it allows the bilirubin to be eliminated.

Obviously, the color of feces or urine will vary based on specific dietary constituents and the degree of hydration, but the characteristic colors of our eliminated wastes are a result of the body's natural cycle of self-renewal.

Urine: What Is It?

Urine is composed of liquid and waste products eliminated from the body via the kidneys. The color of urine will vary depending upon the degree of hydration and also certain medical conditions or medications. The smell of urine can be affected by a variety of foods and spices. As a fertilizer, its NPK rating averages 17-3-3, making it a valuable source of nitrogen. Because of this, in many countries urine is captured in a separate sewage flow. It's hard to guess how much urine people make daily because of the wide variation in personal preferences for hydration, but estimates vary between two and four pounds.

You may recall that earlier in this book, I used gunpowder as a way of illustrating the law of conservation of matter. Because urine is so high in nitrogen, it can be used to make crude potassium nitrate useful for making gunpowder. If urine is mixed with dry hay, dry straw or even dry sawdust and allowed to self-compost for several months, crude potassium nitrate can be derived by pouring boiling water through the mass, filtering, and then evaporating off the water. This is certainly an inefficient way to make gunpowder ingredients, but the crude and impure potassium nitrate obtained is also a fertilizer containing both the potassium and nitrogen needed by plants.

Phosphorus, another key element for plants, was first isolated from urine by Hennig Brand in 1669, and Robert Boyle used a method of combining the solids left after evaporating urine with sand and charcoal and applying heat to separate the elemental phosphorus.

With potassium nitrate and phosphorus supplying all three major macro-nutrients for plants, this illustrates just how much of a nutritional powerhouse urine is for plants.

Urine contains everything eliminated from the body via the kidneys. It contains sugars (hopefully very little unless one is diabetic), salts, urea, proteins, hormones, metabolic by-products of prescription or self-administered drugs and more. Urine from a healthy person is sterile, containing no pathogens and though it is unpalatable, it is considered to be non-toxic. However, once outside the body it will not remain sterile for very long because it is such a rich source of nutrients that microbes will be unable to resist.

Because urine is 94 percent moisture and has a C/N ratio of 0.8, it will compost anaerobically all by itself. This means that it will quickly develop a serious stench as the nitrogen is lost to volatile ammonia. In order to retain the valuable nitrogen and eliminate the stench, urine needs to be combined with a carbon source. In other words, it needs to be aerobically composted. Alternately, urine can be diluted 8:1 with water to be used as a liquid plant food, but as it is low in phosphorus and potassium it shouldn't be used alone unless the latter elements are already present. (I am absolutely NOT endorsing using straight or diluted urine as a plant food, only saying that it CAN be done. The fact is that people consume prescription, over the counter, and illegal drugs like candy in this country, and using straight urine does nothing to mitigate the presence of these drugs and their metabolites, whereas composting the urine will diminish or eliminate them.)

Feces: What Are They?

Other than as an undesired waste product that we flush down the toilet as quickly as possible, few give feces much thought. Most folk think that feces consist mainly of materials that couldn't be digested and couldn't be used by the body. While such materials do indeed make up a portion of feces, what is most surprising to discover is that 80 percent of the dry weight of human feces is composed of bacteria. The NPK value of human feces averages 6-4-2, its C/N ratio averages 7.5 and its moisture content is around 75 percent. How much feces someone makes is largely dependent on how much is eaten, but it is generally estimated that a person makes between a half pound and a pound of feces daily.

It turns out that bacterial cells in our bodies outnumber human cells by 10:1, so the bacteria in our intestines is quite important. Medical science is only beginning to unravel the role our intestinal bacteria play in everything from our dietary preferences to mental states. I have previously described the role bacteria play in helping us eliminate excess bilirubin from the body, but they also help synthesize important vitamins and protect us from less friendly bacterial species. One of the reasons "stomach bugs" are accompanied by diarrhea is that they have evolved a strategy of eliminating friendly bacteria from our intestines so they can have free rein. A round of antibiotics can often cause intestinal symptoms or diarrhea because of imbalances in bacteria until a proper balance is re-established.

Every person's intestinal bacterial profile is unique. The specific bacteria and proportions for a given individual are affected by that person's immune system, environmental exposures and diet. Likewise, because of individual genetic differences and acquired immunities, a bacteria that exists with perfect benignity in one person's gut could cause discomfort to another person. Either way, feces always contain exactly the perfect bacteria to affect their own composting, but even feces from a perfectly healthy person can carry hazards for others.

Unlike urine, feces are far from sterile when they exit the body. Because of their high moisture content and low C/N ratio, they will almost immediately start anaerobic decomposition accompanied by stench and flies. The best way to preserve fecal nutrients while avoiding stench is to combine fecal matter with appropriate materials to compost it aerobically. And the best way to make sure it is bacteriologically safe is to make sure that its aerobic composting is conducted thermophilically. The good news about the non-sterile nature of feces is that, like everything else in nature, they come complete with the precise bacteria best suited for their composting.

Contextualizing the Hazards of Human Waste

What I am describing in this chapter is the use of composting to process human waste that comes *from your own body* and the bodies of people living in close proximity to you – i.e. your family. I am not describing setting up waste collectors in Times Square. This is an important consideration when putting the hazards of the waste you are processing into context.

Bacteria, protozoans, fungi and so forth don't just spontaneously emerge.[48] Rather, they are the offspring of parents like themselves. If the parent is not present, the child will not be created. In other words, you cannot have obligate pathogens[49] in your excrement unless those pathogens are already in your body. All manner of horrible diseases can be spread through human waste, including cholera, shigella, typhoid, intestinal parasites, giardia, amebiasis and hepatitis A among others. But the organisms that cause these diseases don't just magically appear in feces. They would only appear in your waste stream if you *already had them*. This means that unless you are carrying these diseases (which is something you'd usually know), nobody will be able to catch them even by outright eating your manure. (Please don't try this!)

You know the state of your own health, and you know the state of health of the members of your family. If none of your family is sick with something that is spread through feces, then those pathogens won't be present. Period. And even if they

---

48 The theory of spontaneous generation was conclusively disproved by Louis Pasteur in 1859.

49 Sometimes, whether a microbe is pathogenic or not depends on its location. For example, your intestinal bacteria are perfectly fine and safe while in your intestines, but if your intestines were perforated and the bacterial contents spilled into your abdominal cavity, the resulting infection would be life-threatening. An obligate pathogen is a microbe that *only exists as a pathogen* and cannot exist within humans in a way that is not pathogenic. An example would be bubonic plague bacteria.

are somehow present, thermophilic composting will destroy them. Your composted waste is microbiologically safe.

Furthermore, though there is a lot of talk about the presence of heavy metals in sewage sludge; this shouldn't be extrapolated to include human waste you've collected in a bucket for composting. Sewage sludge has passed through *plumbing*. The very word, plumbing, is derived from the Latin word *plumbum*, which means lead. Because of the ease with which it can be sealed, soldered and routed, a great deal of the solder and piping used in sewage piping for hundreds of years has either been made exclusively from lead or has contained lead.

Even modern pipes which contain no lead will contain copper, iron, zinc, nickel or metallic impurities. When someone dumps something acidic such as vinegar down the sink, small portions of these metals will be dissolved and will accumulate in the waste stream. In addition, there are still a tremendous number of homes and apartments that were constructed prior to 1970 and contain lead paints. When the walls and molding in these homes are washed, or when accumulated dust is mopped from the floor then washed down the drain, heavy metals enter the sewage stream. Paris Green and Scheele's Green are pigments containing arsenic that were once used in both wallpaper and printing ink, and washing walls in old homes can therefore introduce arsenic into the waste stream as well.

If the food you eat contains heavy metals, they will be more concentrated in your feces than they are in the food you eat because they are not absorbed well into your body. I've heard of someone becoming so angry he could chew railroad ties and spit nails, but most of us *aren't eating any substantial quantity of heavy metals*. And because you are not eating heavy metals and you are not passing your waste through plumbing, the waste stream that you are composting won't contain them either. In fact, by the time you mix in your brown material in the bucket and other materials in the outdoor pile, any heavy metals present will be no more concentrated than in the food you eat. So there is no hazard from toxic metals.

The question of pharmaceuticals is a bit less cut and dried, simply because there have not been any studies I could find on the fate of pharmaceuticals in thermophilically composted human waste. There have, however, been studies done on sewage sludge, animal carcasses and animal manures as well as composted animal carcasses and manures. Since human beings are mammals, the studies on the fate of pharmaceuticals in composted animal cadavers and composted animal manure are entirely applicable.

National standards allow raw manure to be applied to organic crops at any point more than 120 days from harvest. Though such practices have been shown to be safe from the standpoint of pathogens, veterinary drugs in the raw waste do not break down very well, and can wind up being absorbed into foods such as lettuce.[50] On the other hand, thermophilic composting of animal manures has been demonstrated to reduce levels of antibiotics by as much as 99 percent in as little as twenty-two days.[51] Other studies[52] have shown even greater reductions.

---

50 "Livestock Antibiotics Can End Up in Human Foods", Environmental News Service, 12 July 2007

51 Dollivera, H., Gupta, S. and Noll, S., *Antibiotic Degradation During Manure Composting*, (Wisconsin: University of Wisconsin-River Falls, 2007)

52 Ramaswamy J. et al., "The effect of composting on the degradation of a veterinary pharmaceutical", Bioresource Technology, 107;7 (April 2010): 2294–9

A study of cadavers of horses euthanized via barbiturate overdose showed effective elimination of barbiturate residue via composting[53], and the same study showed effective elimination of NSAIDs.[54]

Livestock used for these studies are typically only exposed to a few classifications of drugs, such as hormones, antibiotics, NSAIDs and barbiturates. Livestock aren't administered entire categories of drugs that humans use routinely, such as antidepressants, statins, opiates, monoamine oxidase inhibitors, recreational drugs and more. As a result, there are no direct studies on their breakdown in compost.

In general, drugs do not exit the body unchanged anyway. Rather, they are detoxified via a variety of mechanisms and what exits our bodies is already broken down to some degree. (This is in general—there are a few drugs that exit exactly as they entered.) When combined with heat and time during composting, most drugs or their metabolic by-products will be degraded into benign substances. However, there is a great deal that is unknown. For example, scientists don't even know what over half of the metabolites of fluoxetine are,[55] so if you don't know what they are, how can you measure them in compost? So my advice, because I cannot give you any assurance of safety with drugs, is if you or a member of your family is taking any drugs other than those shown to break down in

---

53 Hoffmann, M. P., (2012). Assessing the Fate of Drugs in Livestock Mortality and Manures
54 NSAIDs are "Non-Steroidal Anti-Inflammatory Drugs". Common examples include aspirin, acetaminophen, ibuprofen and naproxen.
55 Gram, Lars F., "Drug Therapy: Fluoxetine", *New England Journal of Medicine,* (17 November 1994)

composted animal manure, to only use the resulting compost on ornamental plants and landscaping or to bury it.

Your Emergency Toilet

It's not practical for most people to make a toilet capable of directly thermophilically composting feces because in order to do that, you'd need a toilet holding at least twelve but preferably more than twenty cubic feet of waste, plus the ability to aerate that compost and continue using the toilet while previous feces continue to compost. Such systems are available, but they take up multiple floors and cost thousands of dollars including installation.

What I propose instead is much more simple: put a toilet seat on a five-gallon bucket and every time the bucket is used, add a sufficient quantity of high C/N ratio material to absorb excess moisture, promote aerobic composting and cover the waste so it doesn't stink or attract flies. When the bucket is half full, empty it into an outdoor compost pile dedicated specifically to the purpose of recycling human waste. If the pile doesn't have enough mass to hold thermophilic heat levels, then add sufficient materials in the correct proportions to make it happen.

You can make your emergency toilet as elaborate as you would like, complete with lacquered wood accents, and some people actually do that. But as a standard toilet seat balances fine on a standard five-gallon bucket and this is for emergency use, setting the seat on the bucket works fine. You likely already have a five-gallon bucket, and if you don't, such buckets cost $5 or less. An economy toilet seat costs about $15 at the time of writing, and it fits on a five-gallon bucket perfectly to

» My emergency toilet is in the
woodshed for privacy.
Note that excrement is covered and dry.

make a stool that is the perfect height for ease of use.
Put the seat down when not
in use. If you search the Internet, you'll find that using five-
gallon buckets as toilets is sufficiently common that you can
buy "snap-on" toilet seats customized to fit the buckets at a
reasonable price.

If you have a gift for carpentry, by all means make your
toilet as aesthetically pleasing as you'd like. Make sure your
designs allow the toilet seat to fit against the rim of the bucket
so there is no leakage when people are sitting down and ensure
that the bucket is easily changed without need to tip it.

What to Add to Your Waste

In discussing indoor composting in Chapter 6, we faced
the same problems as with human waste. Specifically, just like
kitchen waste, human waste tends to have a high moisture
content combined with a low C/N ratio that in combination
promotes anaerobic composting, meaning horrendous smells
and attracting a lot of pests. In all fairness, in a natural setting such circumstances wouldn't prevail because waste in the
wild would quickly normalize to the prevailing moisture levels
of the surroundings and so forth. But we don't live under the
bright blue sky, and our population density is such that just
leaving our scat in the woods wouldn't be sustainable.

So, because we have to work with the artificial circumstances of our population density and the fact our waste would necessarily be artificially confined, as it comes from our bodies anaerobic circumstances would prevail. With anaerobic circumstances comes an unsightly, smelly, fly infested mess. The solution, just as with kitchen waste, is to add the right amount of absorbent high-carbon material to allow for aerobic composting. Easy.

In theory, you can add any finely processed "brown" material. Anything that would be readily suitable for mixing with kitchen waste will work for human waste. Examples would include sawdust, dry shredded leaves, ground up hay, peat moss and shredded newspaper.

You want a final C/N ratio of about 30, and the average C/N ratios of urine and feces are 0.8 and 7.5 respectively. The average instance of urination eliminates about a pound of urine and the average act of defecation eliminates about half a pound of feces. Knowing these figures and using the tables and equations from Chapter 3 we can readily calculate the required amounts of brown material that should be added.

Brown Materials Added When the Toilet Is Used		
Material	Amount Added per Urination	Amount Added per Defecation
Dried ground leaves	11 oz (7-2/3 cup)	9 oz (6-1/4 cup)
Hardwood sawdust	2 oz (1-1/4 cup)	1 oz (2/3 cup)
Peat moss	16 oz (4-3/4 cup)	13 oz (3-3/4 cup)
Shredded newspaper	3 oz (10 cups)	2.5 oz (8 cups)

Looking at the accompanying table, it's easy to see that in terms of sheer bulk, hardwood sawdust would be most efficient, except that it won't absorb enough moisture in the case of urine. Peat moss would be great for urine, but would absorb too much moisture for feces. It's a catch-22 because anything that would give you the right C/N ratio in both instances would either absorb too much or too little moisture.

But keep in mind that, within the bucket itself, we are not trying to do composting. Instead, all we are trying to do is avoid anaerobic composting and the accompanying problems with smell and flies. From that perspective, all we really need to do is add enough material to absorb most moisture and make sure the human waste is completely covered after each use. Adding extra material will move it above the thermophilic C/N range of 30, but will also move it well out of the anaerobic range. This is not a problem, because when the bucket is emptied into the outdoor compost pile dedicated to human waste, materials will be added to make up the difference.

When you set up your toilet, you should put a layer of your brown material at the bottom of the bucket, and each time you use it, add enough brown material to absorb moisture and cover the waste. Nothing more elaborate is required until you take the bucket outside.

Composting Human Waste Outside

Unlike the simple compost bins made of chicken wire and stakes that I specified earlier for aerobic composting, human waste has somewhat more elaborate requirements because its leakage, especially in proximity to water supplies, could be a real problem. So unlike standard aerobic compost, you don't want it setting directly on the ground or leaching into the ground.

⊗ Outdoor bin made from pallets. Note that the floor is tilted back and has a lip on the front to prevent liquids from draining onto the ground.

Because I don't compost a lot of human waste, I have only one bin for that purpose that I built from plastic shipping pallets lined with a tarp. The floor of the bin is tilted backward to retard drainage and there is a a lip in front to further prevent it. I screwed it all together with deck screws. There's also a tarp on the top that I install when it rains to keep the pile from overflowing and draining onto the ground. Obviously, I don't use sharp objects in that pile!

⊗ The bin is lined with a tarp to prevent drainage.

Because the amount of brown material added to your emergency toilet will likely make your waste too dry plus it will have too high of a C/N ratio for thermo-philic aerobic composting, you will need to supplement your bin with materials having a lower C/N ratio as

⊗ A tarp covers the bin to keep heavy rains from flooding the bin and causing drainage and anaerobic conditions.

well as watering it. In my experience, you'll need, by volume, about a quarter as much "green" as refuse from your emergency toilet, thoroughly mixed, to create a thermophilic action. If the amount of waste is small, you won't have a large enough pile to retain enough heat for thermophilic composting, so divert materials from your regular aerobic pile as needed until you've accumulated sufficient mass to sustain thermophilic composting.

An easy approach is to add standard composting materials to the bin, then add your human waste, and top it off with enough materials to make a self-sustaining pile.

At that point, you need to manage and turn your pile just as you would a thermophilic aerobic pile because that's exactly what it is. All known human pathogens will be killed in a thermophilic compost pile. At a temperature of 115°F, they will be killed within seven days. At a temperature of 122°F, they will be killed within a day. And at a temperature of 140°F, they will be killed within an hour. For human waste I'd take the National Organic Program standards a bit further because they were only intended for animal wastes. Instead of maintaining a temperature of at least 131°F for at least three days, I would recommend a temperature of at least 140°F for at least five days total, during which the pile has been turned so that everything gets heated through.

Human waste, feces particularly, contains more phytotoxins than animal manure. As a result, it takes longer to cure. After the thermophilic phase has been exhausted, allow the compost to cure for three months, turn it again, and then check it for maturity using the standard radish seed method after another three months.

According to a great many authorities, your compost can now be used on crops intended for human consumption as if it were any other compost. This is not surprising. HOW-EVER, if you intend that your farm be organically certified or want to participate in the Certified Naturally Grown program, no matter how it is processed, *human waste cannot be used on crops*. If you are reticent to use composted human waste on crops, then you can do as I do and use it as a top dressing for ornamental plants.

What if You Can't Compost in an Emergency?

Flies are disease-carriers. They don't have teeth, so in order to eat something, they regurgitate what is already in their stomach onto their new meal to help dissolve it, and then suck it up. If their stomach happens to contain mouldering pestilence, it will be imparted to any food they endeavor to eat. This is why public health codes regulate their presence in restaurants, and a major reason why properly handling human waste in an emergency can spell the difference between self-sufficiency and being a casualty.

If you are already actively composting, it is very easy to take the next step to handle human waste via those methods. But if you don't already have a composting system or the requisite materials and find yourself without power and water due to a hurricane or a citywide grid failure, the midst of a crisis may not be the best time to start thinking about composting human waste.

In addition, when disaster strikes, you might be visiting a friend who lives on the seventeenth floor of a high rise in Chicago and whose facilities for being able to handle such matters are limited.

First thing is first: if there is no water pressure, do not use the toilet. Tape it off and put a sign on it. Though a toilet can be manually flushed by quickly dumping a couple of gallons of water into the bowl from a bucket, in a situation where there is no running water using potable water that way would be wasteful because the water is needed for cleansing and drinking.

If you are in an area that isn't a concrete jungle and you have access to land, then you can use what is called a *cat hole*. A cat hole is nothing more than a 1'-diameter hole dug 6" deep in which you do your business. When done, fill the hole with the dirt you removed while digging. Locate cat holes at least 200' from water sources and well away from evident surface water.

If you will be serving multiple people for what might be longer than a day, you can expand a cat hole into a *trench latrine*. A trench latrine is 1.5' wide, 1' deep, and anywhere from 3'–6' long. As with cat holes, locate trench latrines well away from water sources and obvious surface water. As they are used, keep flies off by shoveling some dirt over the waste. You can erect a frame to facilitate use and provide a privacy barrier. When a trench latrine is no longer needed, fill it in with the dirt you removed while digging it.

If cat holes and trench latrines aren't a viable option and you must stay indoors, then use a plastic garbage bag. You can use use a plunger to remove the remaining water from a toilet and line it with a garbage bag, or you can use the garbage bag to line a bucket. Each time the bag is used, add some absorbent material to cover the waste and keep it from becoming a sloppy, noxious mess. You can use cat litter, paper towels, or even large quantities of toilet paper. Twice a day, tie up the old garbage bag by tying it in a knot so nothing can get in or out and install a fresh bag.

Please note that the determining factor for when to tie up the bag is how long it has been used rather than how full it has become. The bags can be set aside to compost anaerobically for a year and the resulting contents used as a top dressing for ornamental plants, or they can be disposed according to whatever local regulations prevail in your area.

For More Information

The information in this chapter is tailored for composting human waste on an emergency basis because composting it is superior, in terms of sanitation, to what usually happens in circumstances where people have no access to flush toilets. What usually happens is people fill up the toilets in short order, or even start using bare earth indiscriminately. This creates a disease vector as well as a quality-of-life issue. Fortunately, just a little bit of forethought can create superior outcomes.

Composting human waste is not at all limited to emergencies and even the EPA recognizes that composting human waste on an ongoing basis provides an environmentally sound solution that uses less water and returns nutrients to the land. Composting human waste was, at one time, a very controversial subject but is now pretty mainstream. However, if you want to compost human waste on full-time basis you should either use one of the commercial composting toilets or read Joseph Jenkins' *The Humanure Handbook*, in which he describes everything you need to know for handling human waste on that scale.

This chapter gives you what you need in order to handle human waste on a small scale. When the scale is increased to handle full-time human waste disposal, there are a few minor differences—predominantly the need to use multiple buckets indoors and multiple piles outdoors. There are some common-sense and logistical as well as aesthetic issues that become applicable and that Jenkins covers very thoroughly with a lot of helpful suggestions and examples.

10

Sheet Composting/ Lasagna Gardening

One method of composting that is given inadequate attention is sheet composting, which is also called "lasagna gardening" based upon the way the ingredients are layered. Sheet composting is a no-till method that is ideally suited to making raised beds in-place without need for double digging. The only disadvantage is that it can take quite a while to be ready. If you already have a garden or some garden beds in place and you would like to add an additional bed or space, the sheet composting method can be ideal. The best time to prepare a bed is in the late summer or early fall so it will be ready in the spring.

There is one serious limitation to sheet composting that makes it unsuitable in some areas: it does nothing about underlying rocks. There's only one way to get out the rocks: digging. But even for folk who have already double-dug a raised bed, sheet composting can come in handy to boost a bed's fertility or rehabilitate a neglected bed.

How It Works

If you put a layer of leaves on the ground and cover it with snow at 32°F, you might think nothing was going on or that everything would be frozen in stasis until spring . . . but you'd be wrong. Psychrophilic microbes will break down organic matter at temperatures ranging from 0°F to 55°F and provide food for worms at the interface of leaves and soil. Worms, of course, burrow deeper into the ground when it is very cold, but if you'll recall, even in anaerobic conditions where methane is produced rather than carbon dioxide, microbes consuming just one gram of glucose generate enough heat to raise the temperature of 100 pounds of compost by 1.2°F. Any aerobic composting that is occurring generates even more heat, with a single gram of glucose generating enough heat to raise the temperature of 100 pounds of compost by 20°F! In addition, the layers of materials form a layer of insulation between the frigid air and snow and the soil. So your sheet compost is creating an oasis and playground for worms.

Because just plain leaves don't contain enough nitrogen to support a lot of bacterial life, your casual observations would indicate that sheet composting won't work very well.

But you'll be creating a mix of brown and green materials in your bed that will give microbes all the raw material they need, and sheet composting will work far better than you'd expect.

Establishing the Bed

Start by mowing the lawn or cutting the weeds where your bed will be. You don't have to dig up any sod or weeds, just cut them normally. Then, lay out a frame as you would for an ordinary raised bed. I suggest using 2" × 6" lumber because it will contain the pile better, but you can get away with 2" × 4" lumber. I recommend the bed be 8' long, because that's a standard length for dimensional lumber, and anywhere from 3.5'–4' wide for ease of reach because once you build your bed, you never want to walk in it and compact the soil. Just lay the frame on top of the ground.[56] This method relies on earthworms for tillage, so stepping in the bed will undo their hard work.

» This bed was established in poor soil and will be rehabilitated with sheet composting.

Once the frame is laid out, lay either a single layer of over-lapped corrugated cardboard

---

56 You can also use plastic lumber commonly used on decks for a more durable bed frame. You can paint the lumber using exterior latex or exterior acrylic paint and allow it to dry thoroughly before use for a more durable bed, being extra sure to get good coverage of the end-grain. Absolutely *do not use pressure treated lumber* as it has poisons that could leach into the soil and harm either your plants or your family.

or three to five layers of newspaper (omit the glossy inserts) right on the grass or weeds. If you'd like, you can slide them under the boards and even let them stick outside the boards by an inch for greater weed suppression. Once the cardboard or newspapers are in place, wet them down so they sit nice and snug against the grass and weeds to smother them.

⊗ Several layers of wet newspaper cover the surface of the bed.

Your next task is to layer your compost materials one to two feet high in the bed. To keep materials from going outside their designated area or blowing all over the yard,

⊗ The portable posts and the netting can be re-used indefinitely.

I use portable fence posts commonly used for electric fencing that you put into the ground by stepping on a stirrup, and surround them with lightweight plastic poultry netting that can be re-used indefinitely. The posts and netting are removed in the spring.

What to Put on the Bed

This is a mixed mesophilic aerobic and anaerobic pile. As such, its contents should be limited to what you can use in such composts safely. In my area, because the first fall frost is in September and the last winter frost is in May, there is plenty of time for me to safely use animal manures because by applying them in the fall, they would definitely be in place way more than 120 days before any harvest. Take this into account when adding animal manures.

As long as you keep that advice in mind, include anything you'd like to compost, just apply it in alternating layers of brown and green material. I have an electric leaf vacuum that sucks up and shreds leaves, and a lawnmower with a bag. Try to apply two inches of brown material for every inch of green and wet down each layer as it is added. You can include leaves, grass clippings, animal manures, kitchen waste, coffee grounds, bad fruit or vegetables, seaweed, shredded newspaper and just about anything else *except* any more than accidental amounts of animal products such as grease, meat, milk and cheese or vegetable oils.

A layer of lawn clippings goes first.

A layer of sawdust is added.

Chicken manure is added on top of some hay.

Sheet Composting/Lasagna Gardening

The reason for excluding these materials in sheet composting is because while these products can be effectively buried and quickly degraded in a thermophilic pile, this sort of pile is far from thermophilic and won't form an effective biofilter either, so it will attract the attention of unwanted animals to your yard. Where I live, unwanted animals could include raccoons, opossums and black bears. Though black bears are said to fear humans I'd rather not tangle with one if it can be avoided.

I would also recommend avoiding horse manure in particular as an addition to your bed. Horse manure contains a lot of weed seeds that are not broken down adequately by sheet composting. Horse manure is fine in thermophilic compost because the weed seeds are killed, but in sheet composting those seeds will remain and turn your bed into a weed nightmare come spring. If you want to use horse manure, make sure it has already been thermophilically composted. Just because sheet composting is a form of composting doesn't mean you can't add compost made by other methods to the pile. In fact, adding some compost from your other piles made by other methods will definitely be helpful in accelerating the process of sheet composting.

Once you have stacked up one or two feet of material in the bed, go inside, get all snug for the winter, and ignore it until spring. The layer of cardboard or newspaper encourages earthworms in that area, the weight of fall rains or winter snows will keep everything in place, and a mix of microbes will break it down so the earthworms will have a field day.

Planting

Using the sheet composting method, you will be planting directly in compost. As a result, the first year you use the bed,

I would recommend transplanted crops such as tomatoes, cabbage, broccoli and peppers rather than directly seeded crops such as spinach or turnips. The reason is because the compost may be a bit immature and still contain compounds that will suppress seed germination.

If you included animal manures in your layers of compost material, root crops should also be avoided in the first season because manures will cause defects in crops such as carrots and impart a distinctly manure-type flavor to other root crops. After the first year, you can plant anything you'd like in the bed and it should sprout, grow and taste just fine!

The newspaper or cardboard may not degrade completely the first year, and neither will the top layer added to your sheet compost. If it hasn't, that's not a problem – punch through it with your trowel when adding transplants.

Maintenance

I cover the maintenance of raised beds in terms of cover cropping, crop rotations, and similar practices pretty thoroughly in my book *Mini Farming: Self Sufficiency on ¼ Acre*. However, there is no reason why you can't use sheet composting to maintain a bed. To do so, put your poles and netting around the bed and add your layers right on top of the soil just as you did when the bed was established the first time. The only proviso is that anytime you do that, you'll have to skip directly seeded crops and possibly root crops (if animal manures were used) in the subsequent growing season.

The single most important factor in maintaining raised beds is to avoid stepping on them. These beds are rich in organic matter, so earthworms do your tilling for you. Because of the high earthworm populations, the soil is maintained with a beautiful structure that allows for proper aeration, moisture and drainage without a need for back-breaking work with a tiller. If you go stomping around on your beds you will cancel that advantage.

11

Compost Tea

If you are familiar with organic gardening, you have probably heard of compost tea as well as its benefits in enhancing crop growth and yield along with disease suppression[57]. The theory is that compost tea works as a foliar spray by putting beneficial microbes on the plants that will either compete against or crowd out pathogens plus add beneficial microbes and nutrients

---

57 From the Compost Tea Industry Association website at http://www.composttea.org

to the soil. It is also theorized that nutrients in compost tea, including humic acids and humic acid chelates, are bio-available via foliar application and enhance the health of plants through stimulating growth and immune response.

Some Science Regarding Compost Tea

Some of the literature extolling the virtues of compost tea resembles the wonder claims of nineteenth century snake-oil salesmen, which should raise suspicion. The reality is that the results of studies vary widely, ranging all the way from useless to helpful, but none of them support the notion of compost tea as something that works wonders. Improved growth and yield is the most consistent result, and suppression of powdery mildew is commonly noted, but these results are anecdotal.

Linda Chalker-Scott, Associate Professor of Horticulture and Landscape Architecture at WSU, having examined the available evidence has concluded: "In a scientific nutshell, there is no solid evidence to support use of compost tea, particularly aerated compost tea, in disease suppression. Likewise, there is no evidence to support a nutritional role ..."[58]

In 2001, Cascadia Consulting Group conducted compost tea trials for the City of Seattle on roses to see if compost tea had any beneficial effect on a number of diseases including black spot and powdery mildew, and found no benefit.[59]

---

58 Chalker-Scott, Linda, *Parking Tickets, Compost Tea and Pseudoscience in the Ivory Tower* (Washington State University, 2011)
59 Cascadia Consulting Group, Compost Tea Trials, Final Report, (March 2001)

If you think about it, one of the benefits of compost is that it binds nutrients in an insoluble form that won't be washed out of the soil and can be made available to plants via microbial mediation on an as-needed basis. If the nutrients are insoluble, then by definition most of them cannot be extracted into tea. Naturally, some *small* portion of the nutrients will be dissolved and made available to plants in the tea, but most of the nutrients will remain behind in solid form. The only way they would be available would be in the cytoplasm of microorganisms that have multiplied during the tea's manufacture.

As for the beneficial bacteria and fungi, when you spray them on your plant foliage they will be exposed to sunlight and copious amounts of ultraviolet radiation. I use an ultraviolet sanitizer to indiscriminately kill bacteria in my water supply. It works impressively well. Though some of the fungi in compost tea may escape death from sunshine and those bacteria that can hide underneath the leaves may prosper, the overwhelming preponderance of the microbes sprayed on the foliage will be killed and therefore cannot provide any benefit.

It also stands to reason that if compost tea is what you want, spreading the compost on the ground where aerated rain water will percolate through it and carry the tea into the soil immediately would work pretty well. Meanwhile, earthworms would appreciate the organic matter.

So basic knowledge of compost, microbes and sunshine backs up Professor Chalker-Scott's analysis, at least in terms of applying compost tea as a spray to plants. However, the product is far from useless. One area in which compost tea has been scientifically demonstrated to be very useful is when tea made from vermicompost is applied as a soil drench (i.e. it is used to water the plants).[60] Furthermore, when applied as a soil drench the microbes (and the nutrients they contain) would be washed down into the soil where they would be protected from ultraviolet light.

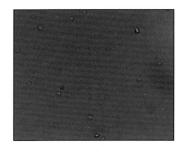

⊗ Bacterial population in a poor raised bed before being drenched with compost tea.[61]

In my own tests of same-species plants in the same bed, soil drenches with compost tea DO enhance growth and disease resistance, but foliar sprays have no measurable effect. The benefits are only apparent in my beds with the poorest fertility. Most of my beds are very fertile and the compost tea has no discernible benefit on plants grown in them. But as I mentioned, it has benefit for plants in my least fertile beds, so my own recommendation is to use it as a soil drench in newly established garden areas until they have reached a high level of fertility.

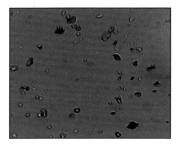

⊗ Bacterial population in the same bed two weeks after being drenched with compost tea.

60 Edwards, C. et al., "Effect of aqueous extracts from vermicomposts on attacks by cucumber beetles on cucumbers and tobacco hornworm on tomatoes", *Pedobiologia*, (August 2009)
61 Five grams of soil were shaken in a test tube with 30 ml of water and allowed to settle. A drop of the liquid was spread on a slide, allowed to dry, heat fixed over flame then stained for two minutes with methylene blue. Irregular dark specks in the photo are microscopic soil particles.

The results of testing compost tea would naturally be inconsistent because the product itself embodies so many variables in its manufacture that controlling for them would be nearly impossible. There are differences in the ingredients, differences in the aging, differences in the aeration, differences in the proportions of compost and timing of aeration and so forth. There would also be differences in results if it is sprayed during a period of cloudy weather as opposed to bright sun, or applied in the evening so it can work overnight as opposed to morning when it will be degraded by sunshine all day. Whether you decide to try compost tea or not is up to you. What I am going to describe in this chapter is best practices that will improve your odds of a beneficial result while minimizing the odds of creating a product that will do harm or spread illness.

What Kind of Compost Is Best for Tea?

You can make compost tea from any sort of compost, including anaerobic, aerobic and vermicompost. The substances used to make the compost make a difference in its effectiveness. Specifically, compost that includes animal manures as a feedstock performs better. In addition, aerobic compost and vermicompost work better than anaerobic compost. If using compost that included animal manures, for reasons of safety, it *must* have been processed thermophilically with adequate turning to assure pathogen death. Otherwise, you could be spraying E. coli or salmonella all over your crops with devastating consequences.

So for best results, use thermophilic compost that included animal manures. Mesophilic aerobic compost and vermicompost are also good choices. Last place goes to anaerobic compost.

The age of compost used to make tea also affects its effectiveness. Any compost used needs to have been cured sufficiently to pass the radish test, because otherwise you could be defeating your own purpose by spraying your crops with phytotoxins. At the same time, the compost should not have been curing for more than nine months because compost much older than that isn't as reliably useful for compost tea.

How Long Should the Tea Be Aerated?

Compost can be mixed with water, allowed to steep for a couple of hours without aeration and then filtered. The result is called *compost extract*. As long as it is only steeped a couple of hours and then used immediately, it will be as safe to use as the compost from which it is made. However, if steeped any longer, any aerobic organisms will be killed and anaerobic organisms will be favored, so it shouldn't be used directly on foliage unless it is applied 120 days or more before harvest.

When you aerate the mixture of compost and water, the result is called *compost tea*. When you are using aerobic compost, whether mesophilic or thermophilic, as well as vermicompost, you only need to steep with aeration for one or two days because you are starting out with a high population of aerobic microbes. But if the compost you are using has cured for more than nine months or it was produced anaerobically, then the period of aeration will need to extend for five to eight days in order to build up the aerobic organisms that make compost tea effective.

The degree of aeration required can be best approximated by that required in an aquarium. You want at least one liter of air per minute per five gallons. Using more air is perfectly fine as the absorption capacity of water is such that it can't absorb enough air to hurt anything, so I err on the safe side by injecting between two and a half and three liters of air per minute for five gallons of water.

Additives for Compost Tea

The standard recommendation from many county extension services is to add a bit[62] of unsulfured molasses to compost tea as it brews in order to give food to the beneficial microbes. Such advice seems to have worked well as there have been no reports of illness from following that advice.

However, if you are going to add molasses or any other simple sugar, I suggest that you treat the resulting compost tea *as though it were made from raw animal manure* in terms of timing its use because there is no guarantee that the only organisms being fed are beneficial and benign. For short brewing cycles of one or two days starting with aerobic compost or vermicompost, there is no need for such additives so it is best to avoid them and err on the safe side.

The only other thing to watch is chlorinated water. Chlorinated water could kill the beneficial microbes. If your water is chlorinated, aerate it for two hours before use to get rid of

---

62 One tablespoon per five gallons

the chlorine and it will work fine. Obviously, any water used to brew compost tea should be potable.

Your Compost Tea Brewer

There are a number of commercial compost tea systems on the market, but on the scale of a home garden or mini farm, especially given the current state of science regarding compost tea, I don't see buying such a system as justified. It is easy and inexpensive to make compost tea with parts from the hardware and pet store. The system demonstrated cost less than $20.

Materials

> 1 × 5-gallon bucket
> 1 × old pillowcase, the more threadbare the better
> 1 × aquarium aerator (any size from 5–20 gallons)
> 1 or 2 × check valves (included with aerator)
> 1 or 2 × aeration stones
> 8' aquarium air hose, standard size

Procedure

1. Cut the hose to the lengths required for your set up and attach the hose from the aeration stones to the check valves, ensuring the arrows on the check valves are pointing in the direction of air flow.

⊗ Inexpensive aquarium supplies are sufficient to make your own compost tea.

⊗ The completed tea maker.

⊗ How to arrange the pillow case.

⊗ Use a knot easily untied so you can re-use your pillowcase many times as long as you wash and dry it after each use.

2. Cut additional lengths of hose needed to attach the check valves to the aeration pump.
3. Place the aeration stones in the bottom of your bucket.
4. Arrange your pillow case in the bucket as though it were a trash bag in a trash can.
5. Place one shovel full of compost in the pillow case.
6. Use string to tie the pillow case shut.
7. Fill the bucket most of the way with water.
8. Turn on the pump and allow to bubble for the requisite length of time.
9. Turn off the pump, remove the pillowcase filled with compost and empty the compost
10. Use immediately. Once aeration is removed the aerobic bacteria and fungi die quickly.

❯❯ If the compost tea will be used as a foliar spray, use potable water for brewing.

Smell It!

The nose knows. When your compost tea is done brewing, give it the sniff test. If it smells like fresh dirt, it is properly brewed. But if it smells putrid, rotten or otherwise yucky, don't put it on your plants. Your nose is imperfect, but it was designed by nature to help keep you safe. If what you brewed smells unsafe, it probably is – so discard it. The odds of this happening if you have followed the directions and recommendations in this chapter are very low, but it never hurts to give things a final check just in case.

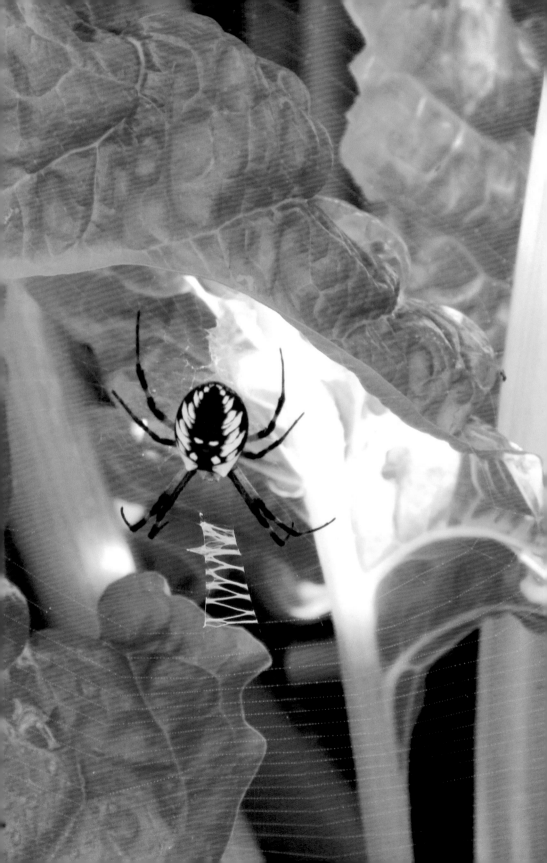

12

Composting for All

Compost improves the aeration and water-holding capacity of the soil, provides beneficial bacteria, reduces the need for fertilizer and enhances plant immunity to pests and diseases. Composting is important. In fact, in terms of the success of your garden, it is the single most important aspect of keeping your costs low, keeping your plants healthy and making the food you grow healthful. Though I cover other important practices such as cover cropping, crop rotation and pest management in other books, without composting the effectiveness of everything else is radically diminished.

Making your own compost makes sense because the cost of bagged compost is too high to be practical for gardens larger than a postage stamp and the quality of compost delivered by the truckload is unreliable. Making your own compost saves money and gives you a product of known quality.

The method of composting described in most books is thermophilic aerobic composting. It is my own preferred method as well, because you can use it to compost everything from corn stalks to manure to chicken carcasses safely. However, thermophilic aerobic composting can be both time consuming and physically demanding; both of which factors can make it a non-starter for many people who are either extremely busy or have physical limitations. The use of tools such as soil augers can help mitigate the physical requirements, but it is still not a spectator sport.

Thankfully, there is more than one road to any given destination. In the previous chapters I have described the reasons why you should make compost, how composting works, the role of compost in the nutrient cycle and how to get your garden soil into the best possible condition for growing. Along with this, I have explained a variety of techniques for making compost aerobically or anaerobically, including indoor methods and vermicomposting.

Everyone should be able to compost in some way. If you live in a community that charges you by the bag for your garbage, even if you don't have and don't want a garden, composting your kitchen wastes and then disposing of the compost in your lawn will save you money and save space in landfills. You can use both the indoor mesophilic composting system and the vermicomposting methods I have described. Of course, if you DO have a garden, both of these approaches will allow you to have compost available when you are starting seedlings in the early spring instead of cursing your frozen compost pile. If even these systems can't be maintained because you have frequent absences, you can use the various anaerobic methods instead.

If you only have one weekend a year to deal with compost, you can make the wet anaerobic digester in minutes, stuff it full of compostable material, cover the material with water and affix the lid . . . then come back several months later to finished compost without any intervention on your part in the interim.

I have also covered the third-rail of composting: human waste. I'm not saying you should necessarily compost all your waste, but want you to know how it can be done in the event of a natural disaster or other problem that stops the never-ending spigots in our homes from running.

Finally, I've demonstrated how you can make your own compost tea.

So what's my point? My point is that composting is accessible to everyone. Whether you are living in a Manhattan high rise, on a farm, or have a small garden in the suburbs, you can compost. Some form of composting is within your capacity whether you live a leisurely lifestyle or are almost never home, whether you are a fitness model or have serious physical limitations. I've seen a ton of books, websites and pamphlets stuffed with all manner of elaborate (and expensive) composting systems that make it seem as though being a master carpenter is a prerequisite to composting, but in this book I have shown how to make durable aerobic composting bins of practically any size inexpensively, how to make anaerobic digesters for $20, how to make your own compost tea brewing system for under $30 and how to make vermicompost bins for less than $10. The most expensive system in this book is a rotating drum composter for indoor use, and complete with paint it costs less than $50. In other words, composting in some form or fashion is entirely financially feasible and any economic barriers are entirely artificial.

A lot of people are intimidated by compost. Next to canning, it is the self-sufficiency skill generating the most apprehension. Anywhere I go to speak, people ask about compost and the questions most often asked pertain to safety. There is no reason to be intimidated and I hope that if you have ever been intimidated by composting, this book has dispelled any reservations you've had. Composting is nothing more than applying a bit of knowledge regarding nature to help natural processes along. Keep in mind what I discussed in the first chapter: nature is on your side and it is almost impossible to mess up so badly that you don't get some sort of compost from your efforts.

So now I'm going to stop writing so you can stop reading and start composting! Good luck!

Index

Notes